As a man who did not have ~~[obscured]~~ when I was young, I have spent much of my adult life trying to learn what it means to be a man who follows Jesus. Frankly, I have learned best from books written long before this present generation, with only a few exceptions. Dr. Brower has written one stunning exception. This book was significantly formative for me as a man who struggles with fear. It magnified Jesus and charted a course for me to follow as one who prays to be a man of God. I recommend this book both to Christian fathers, sons, pastors, and church members, and to cynics about the faith and inquirers into the truths of Christianity. There is much here for the teachable reader. Read slowly and savor carefully. You will not be disappointed.

—**Joe Novenson**, Senior Pastor, Lookout Mountain Presbyterian Church, Lookout Mountain, Tennessee

In a culture of perpetual adolescence, young men need wise guides and wise guidebooks. Shawn Brower has a proven track record not only as a coach and Christian school leader but as a wise guide for young men, and *We Became Men* is a wise guidebook that you'll want to pick up, read, and use whether you are a young man looking for sage counsel or someone older looking to influence the emerging generation. The teaching here is clear, biblical, practical, and visionary. Many lives have been shaped for the better by Shawn, and I pray many more will be shaped because of his important book.

—**John Stonestreet**, Executive Director, Summit Ministries; Director of Strategic Partnerships, Colson Center for Christian Worldview

Shawn Brower knows young men. Athletic coach extraordinaire, he gets inside their heads and inside their hearts. In

We Became Men, young men will be challenged to step up to the plate of their calling, to press onward toward the goal of their purpose in life, and to run the race set before them and already accomplished through the triumph of their gracious Redeemer, the Lord Jesus Christ. Here's the perfect gift for every teen young man.

—**Douglas Bond**, Author, *STAND FAST In the Way of Truth* and *HOLD FAST In a Broken World*

"Do I have what it takes?" This is the question that either motivates or haunts every man. It has motivated Shawn Brower, compelling him to write this amazingly insightful work, and I am here to testify that the stories, insights, and wisdom of the following pages are not theoretical. They are the consummation of a life lived in the uncertain, risky, exhilarating challenge of training boys to become men and to know they have what it takes. . . . So spend some time with Shawn Brower, and discover "a young man's journey to his true masculine design."

—**Bryant Black,** former naval officer, history teacher, and coach

What is genuine masculinity? Could you define it? Could you plot a course and lead others toward the discovery of manhood? For every image of a truly heroic man, we have been given thousands of misrepresentations of what it really means to be a man according to our Creator's design. If you are looking for a book to help you or your youth ministry discover and articulate what authentic manhood is—you have found it! Shawn writes with clear and unvarnished biblical accuracy. Throughout the book he weaves in his own journey and includes noteworthy coaches, teachers, and fathers who most of us can relate to. He also introduces us to a host of biblical characters as well as bringing to the table some of the great classic authors like Calvin, Tolkien, C. S. Lewis, Thoreau, and Shakespeare.

Brower gives us a sharp reminder that man has a propensity for "passivity." We need leaders! Where have the godly men gone? Don't just buy this book, but read it, live it, and teach it!

> —**Steve Connor**, Linebacker, the Chicago Bears and the Los Angeles (now St. Louis) Rams; Founder, Sports Outreach International

Young men, if you are up for a challenge, read this book! Brower challenges us to step up and take *responsibility*—for our hearts, souls, and lives—under the authority of God's Word. This is a great read for young men who are seeking to live truly (and biblically) masculine lives in service to the Lord Jesus Christ.

> —**Jon Nielson,** Pastor for Senior High, College Church, Wheaton

WE BECAME
MEN

WE BECAME MEN

The Journey into Manhood

SHAWN BROWER

PUBLISHING

P.O. BOX 817 • PHILLIPSBURG • NEW JERSEY 08865-0817

Printed in the United States of America

Library of Congress Control Number: 2012937660

#2869   9781596383869
27 Jun 2013

To my three sons: Joshua, Josiah, and Jakob.
I love you deeply! In your journey toward manhood,
may you each find your place in God's kingdom.

CONTENTS

CONTENTS

ACKNOWLEDGMENTS

I FIRST ACKNOWLEDGE my wife and the love of my life for being graciously supportive and willing to join me in the many ventures and adventures we have pursued together. Specifically, she has been a constant source of encouragement throughout the process of writing this book and is the best partner I could ask for in raising our three sons to pursue manhood.

Special thanks to my father, who models what it means to be a real man who follows hard after the heart of God, and to my mother who alongside him has modeled what a Christian marriage and home should be with God and his word as the centerpiece!

Thanks to Forrest Walker, who on receiving each chapter I wrote, provided the feedback of an eternal optimist. His "Barnabus" approach compelled me to continue to write to completion. Words can't express my gratitude for him and the vital role he served.

Thanks to Pastor Joe Novenson, whose humility is otherworldly and whose constant encouragement and shepherding has given me a glimpse of what Timothy must have felt under the care of the apostle Paul.

Thanks to college soccer coach Dave Murray, who showed me what it means to mentor and to disciple men of character and integrity. His willingness to speak hard truths in love and to uncover and develop the strengths in others has motivated me to do no less.

Thanks to Marvin Padgett and all the folks at P&R Publishing for giving me this opportunity to be a published author with them. Finally, a special thanks to Amanda Martin, my editor, who got "stuck" with the rookie writer.

FOREWORD

"DO I HAVE WHAT IT TAKES?" This is the question that either motivates or haunts every man. It has motivated Shawn Brower, compelling him to write this amazingly insightful work, and I am here to testify that the stories, insights, and wisdom in the following pages are not theoretical. They are the consummation of a life lived in the uncertain, risky, exhilarating challenge of training boys to become men and to know they have what it takes.

Seven years ago, the Lord introduced me to this man of passion, integrity, and vigor. You could see it, you could feel it, and you certainly experienced it. That first summer, I invited Shawn and his son Josh to join my son and me on a soccer team for seven- and eight-year-olds on Lookout Mountain, Tennessee. I found a kindred spirit as I watched this father of three sons coach his oldest son and my second of three sons on the "field of battle."

Our boys thrived, and a friendship developed on the field that summer that has translated into a life dedicated to helping our sons and their teammates become young men living in their "true masculine design." It has not been easy. The road less traveled never is. But, it has been worth every trial and tribulation. My oldest son is a senior and a four-year member of Shawn Brower's varsity soccer squad. He has become a man of God, and, in no small measure, this is the consequence of his time with Shawn Brower.

11

Spend some time with Shawn Brower, and discover a young man's journey toward manhood and his true biblical masculine design. Invite another young man or group of guys to read this book together, and, if you do, be vulnerable, honest, and forthright with yourself and the others. In so doing, you choose the narrow path less traveled, "for the gate is narrow and the way is hard that leads to life, and those who find it are few" (Matt. 7:14 ESV).

Bryant Black
Chattanooga, TN

INTRODUCTION

"I SURE WISH someone had told me these things when I was in high school."

These words from a colleague gripped and chilled me. Questions filled my mind. What if other men were thinking similar thoughts and struggling in the same way? What role could I take in this situation? What responsibility did I have to help them?

The questions demanded action. I knew what I needed to do.

It began on September 13, 2010, when I spoke at our school's annual three-day senior retreat. We had taken more than a hundred seniors to a camp in East Tennessee, ferrying them across a lake on pontoon boats to a remote site in the Cherokee National Forest. As we arrived at the secluded campsite, the breathtaking beauty and serenity of this special haven invited us into unfamiliar territory. The natural surroundings allowed teachers and students alike to hear and listen in ways life's rhythm and pace doesn't often allow.

After a great first evening, we awoke to a crisp fifty-degree fall day. Students had been invited to an optional pre-breakfast time of devotions on the boat dock. As I walked down to the dock, the fog slowly lifted off the water, giving way to the sun that peered over the tops of the mountains. Nothing disturbed the water's glassy surface but an occasional fish jumping to secure its morning breakfast.

13

Over half the senior class chose to attend our time of reflection on God's word, and I came away encouraged and uplifted by the students' responsiveness. Yet that memorable beginning was not the defining moment of that day.

After a series of meetings and activities, we entered a late morning, gender-separated session where adult leaders had the opportunity to speak into the lives of the seniors. Since I had led the guys' session for the previous five years, the senior class sponsor had asked me to lead it once again. I had readily agreed, because little in life gives me as much satisfaction and delight as investing in the lives of young men.

At this particular retreat, I spoke on true biblical masculinity and our God-given design as men. I started by asking those robust, highly energized, and testosterone-filled seventeen- and eighteen-year-olds, "How many of you consider yourselves a man?"

Their response, or lack thereof, was telling but not startling. Out of fifty guys, only four raised their hands.

I followed up by asking those four students how they knew they were men. When no response came, I asked a less personal question: "What does it take to be a man?" There was a smattering of answers from the group. Overall, however, confusion and lack of clarity marked those few moments.

After a well-received presentation and an even better discussion with the fifty seniors, comments from two of my peers struck me in a way that propelled me to write this book. As I finished the session, a teacher in his early thirties rose to speak. He had been listening intently to my message, and I was curious to hear what he would say.

"Guys, this is powerful stuff that I personally have never heard before," he said. "Already I'm thinking of how I can apply this to my life today. I sure wish someone had told me these things when I was in high school."

After the retreat, I happened to speak to one of the other leaders, also in his early thirties. He exclaimed, "As a teenager, I'd have practically given my right leg to have heard what you shared with our senior guys!"

On hearing these words, I knew what I needed to do. The students' lack of understanding of their true masculinity, coupled with the words of those highly respected teachers, fueled my passion to specifically speak into the lives of young men. I want to show them the path toward their true masculine design: a journey that brings meaning and purpose to life.

That night, with deep conviction and a clear mission, I set out on that journey with pen in hand.

Young men, I invite you to embark on a journey of hope, direction, and freedom. Let's begin together!

PART 1

BASE CAMP

> "Then Peter got down out of the boat, walked on the water and came toward Jesus."
>
> —*Matthew 14:29*

STAY HOME?

* Discovering your masculine design requires stepping away from false safety and security.
* Journeys filled with adventure and risk lead to personal discovery and revelation.

OCTOBER 24, 1997, is a day forever etched in my memory. On that day, a match between two high-school varsity teams determined which would be the #1 seed going into the state soccer tournament. At the time, I was coaching a team ranked #2 in the state of Florida. We were on a collision course with St. Stephens, the #1 ranked team. To top it off, we would be playing the match on our home field. We always played well at home, so we liked the opportunity before us.

The buildup to that match had the feel of a post-season play-off game. I was interviewed by the newspaper and local news station. We trained hard and prepared well, seeing this as an opportunity to make our mark as we headed into post-season play, set to begin just one week afterward.

Friday morning, the guys had a hard time focusing on school; they just wanted to push through the day and get to the big match. When the moment finally arrived, they played valiantly. However, St. Stephens capitalized early in the match, putting our boys down 0-1. Soon after, St. Stephens struck again, set on proving it really was the top team.

Although they found themselves in a deep hole, our boys refused to lie down and quit. Showing great character and resolve, our team evened the score 2-2 with only ten minutes to play.

With both teams pressing hard, and minutes left on the game clock, St. Stephens struck that decisive goal and held on for the victory.

The night held an even greater test for the guys, however. As evening approached, the entire team, including many parents, came to see me in the hospital. You see, I never attended the game I just described. On that day, my wife gave birth to my firstborn son.

You might imagine the emotions that swirled about in the hospital room. The guys walked in with long faces and began to stammer out apologies. "Coach, we are so sorry we didn't win this game. We wanted to win it for you on this special day."

I interrupted them. "Hey, I don't want to hear another word of it! I have a *son!* Let's celebrate!"

Some of you might be thinking it's too bad I wasn't able to coach that game. First, however, I am convinced the team could not have played any harder had I been present. Second, I humbly confess that earlier in the week I had tried to work this problem out. Pay attention here, because this is something you might read in a book called *Marriage for Dummies*. It could be on the top-ten list of boneheaded mistakes husbands make when their wives are pregnant.

That Thursday morning, I got a call from my wife who was at the doctor's office, getting a checkup to see how the baby was doing.

When I answered the phone, she told me, "The doctor is concerned because the baby is ten to twelve pounds." (If you don't know, that is a big baby.) "He thinks we should have the baby this weekend."

"Wow, that is big . . . but great! So, are we scheduled for this on Saturday?"

"No, more like tomorrow."

Without hesitating, and obviously without thinking a single rational thought, I said, "But we play St. Stephens tomorrow, so just ask the doc if he can do it on Saturday." In my mind, I was thinking, "What is one day when it's been in there for nine months?"

For the next ten seconds, some muffled discussions took place on the other end of the line. Finally, my wife said, "Shawn, the doctor would like to speak with you."

I had never been in trouble with a doctor before, but it felt like being called to the principal's office. While I don't know exactly what the doctor and my wife said in that brief exchange, I remember the only peace I felt was that this was a telephone conversation and not a face-to-face meeting with the two of them. Realizing I was rapidly getting myself into a serious mess, I backtracked and agreed that Friday was a great day—in fact, the best day—to have that big healthy baby!

That Friday ended up being one of the best days of my life. When my wonderful and gracious wife gave birth to our son Joshua Samuel, October 24, 1997, became a day of great remembrance for me.

From that day forward, Joshua has been part of every team I have coached. As a baby, he and my wife would ride on the team bus. As soon as he could walk, he sat on the bench at every game. By the time he was five, he knew every player's jersey number and the position he played. He considered himself one of the guys in every way.

During the summer of 2002, I took my high school soccer team to the mountains of North Carolina for a weeklong, high-country adventure. It had become our custom to spend intentional time together, away from the bright lights and fast pace of Orlando. Our goal was to learn more about each other and ourselves as we collectively experienced adventure in the mountains, rivers, and trails. We wanted to become a true band of brothers with much more in common than just playing soccer together.

When five-year-old Josh heard I was taking a weeklong trip to the mountains of North Carolina with the soccer players and he was going to have to stay at home, he began to posture and position himself in such a way that I soon considered taking him along with us. Although my wife was initially rather reticent to let him accompany us on the journey, we both agreed it would be a good experience for him.

For Josh, this was much more than a trip with Dad: it was as though he were going on a journey with twenty of his older brothers! How could this possibility end with the decision "not this time, son"? How could he stay home without Dad and his twenty "brothers"?

Needless to say, Josh made the trip roster.

THE FIRST STEPS

Eight years later, I asked Josh what he remembered about the trip. I was absolutely amazed when he recounted it like it had happened yesterday. He listed detail after detail: how we got out of bed very early, how one of the players was injured and had to go to the hospital and then use crutches, how we pulled over to the side of the road to jump into a rushing mountain river, and how he was third of all the guys to reach the top of our mountain climb. He even remembered the bagels we ate for breakfast.

As I listened to him retell this trip in such detail, I was struck by how much those experiences had meant to him at such a young age and how they had shaped him into the man he was becoming. He didn't merely recall small details—I heard in his voice the excitement and passion to find his way back into the wild.

What if I had told him he couldn't go? As his dad, I am sure I could have given him good reasons for staying at home. I even agree that the age of five is rather young for such an adventure. However, I took a worthwhile risk, knowing there would be many times during the trip when Josh would see his dad and the players pursuing their masculine design. I wanted him to watch and learn and someday follow in our footsteps.

That experience afforded Josh the gift of watching young men pursue worthy endeavors that required discipline, hard work, commitment, dedication, and perseverance. More importantly, he saw what it meant to be a young man pursuing the heart of God. He remembered how much he had wanted a copy of the notebook and devotional outlines I had prepared for each of the players so they could journal throughout the week. With a smile on his face, Josh recalled his excitement when I pulled out the notebook that would be his own. As the players wrote in their journals, Josh wrote too, creating his own words and deciphering them for me because he did not yet know how to spell. In every way, he wanted to be like those guys.

Maybe most important of all, Josh was not just told or shown the worthy steps he should take. Instead, he was given permission to take his own risks with his dad nearby, to measure himself against the big boys, to hear words of encouragement

23

as he successfully completed a five-mile hike, to hear God's word declared and discussed, and to know what good hard work felt like by the time his head hit the pillow at the end of the day.

Although my son could never have verbalized it at the age of five, he was taking mighty steps in his journey toward manhood. No, to stay home was not an option! Nor has it been an option for him since. Josh has been on well over a dozen expeditions and is begging for more at the age of fourteen! Every trip taken, every adventure pursued, every risk embraced, and every lesson learned has revealed more and more about his heart and his masculine design.

FALSE SAFETY AND SECURITY

For some readers, the idea of going on an outdoor expedition is the last thing on your mind. You have not been invited on such a journey, and you hope the invitation never arrives. You may well find yourself in the safety and security of your home. You have your music, your TV, your Facebook account, your soft warm bed, and the comforts and familiarity of your own room.

While there is nothing inherently wrong with any of those comforts, I ask you, "How are these things preparing you for what is to come?"

Maybe this story will help you to get off the couch.

In Matthew 14, after Jesus had been preaching to the crowds, he sent his disciples ahead of him to the other side of the lake. As they sailed across the lake, a storm began to brew. For the next nine hours, they battled the winds and waves. Exhausted, enveloped in darkness, and having traveled only three miles, they got a break they were not expecting. Looking across the waves, they saw a figure moving toward them—Jesus walking across the water.

When Peter asked the Lord's permission to step out of the boat into the rough waters, Jesus granted him the wish of a lifetime. Peter did what no sinful man had done before or has done since: he walked on water!

The thrill factor of Peter walking on water is not the crux of the story, even though that is a story in itself. My first major observation is *how* Peter found himself walking on the water. He made a deliberate decision to leave the safety of the boat he and the other disciples had depended on for the last nine hours. He entered the complete unknown, where trust and utter reliance on Jesus were an absolute must for any hope of survival!

Jesus knew how important it was for Peter to leave what appeared to be a sure thing: a boat in the middle of a stormy lake. He knew Peter needed to enter a far greater story by stepping into the unknown, fixing his eyes on Jesus, and failing the test—as he did when his doubts caused him to panic and sink into the water. Far greater challenges awaited him. In the middle of that storm, the King of creation rescued Peter from his false security, saving him not just from a watery grave but also from his self-reliance. Peter needed to learn these early lessons in order to enter the greater journey to which Jesus had called him.

GREAT EXPECTATIONS?

Unfortunately, the majority of young men have never been invited to step away from their place of security. Many young men have no sense of urgency to grow up, let alone engage in an adventure that will stretch them in places where they are ill equipped. For some, this journey may include elements that are physically challenging and even dangerous. However, every young man can pursue the heart of the journey regardless of his athletic prowess, because this journey requires more from within than from without.

Can you imagine the intestinal fortitude Peter must have had to step out of the boat? Yes, the Lord was calling to him, and, yes, his actions required a lot of faith—but it also took great guts for Peter to step wildly out of his comfort zone!

You must battle within yourself to release your white-knuckled grip on what is most comfortable. If we were honest with ourselves, most of us would agree that the unfamiliar might be even better than the familiar—yet we would rather hold onto the familiar with deathlike fervor because going into the unknown is just too alarming. If you are willing to let go and venture away from the places where you have often run for safety, you just might discover that the more comfortable you get with being uncomfortable, the faster you will grow as you journey into manhood.

In their book *Do Hard Things*, twin brothers Alex and Brett Harris make a similar point when they note that the teen years are viewed as some sort of a vacation, not a time of risk-taking. "Society does not expect much of anything from young people during their teen years except trouble. And it certainly does not expect competence, maturity or productivity. The saddest part of that, as the culture around has come to expect less and less, young people have dropped to meet those lower expectations."[1]

In 1927, President Bernard Iddings Bell of Saint Stephen's College was troubled by the same issue:

> We are sending forth graduates with diffused minds, scarcely fit to take command of their own lives or to coop-erate in the development of a social state; drifters into conformity and essential human futility, easy victims to specious crowd psychologies: followers of what seem easy ways out. They do the things that will make one comfort-able or popular. Out of our most able youth, capable of

high adventure, we are manufacturing mental and ethical jellyfish.[2]

Unfortunately, part of the problem may have resulted from the lack of a system today that clearly outlines steps toward true masculinity or manhood. As a result, many young men are left to figure out what it means to be a man and to decide for themselves when they have arrived. Inconsistency, lack of good examples, and unanswered questions rule the day, leaving young men to guess if manhood is when they get their driver's license, achieve the legal drinking age, have sex for the first time, head to college, graduate from college, get their first job, get married, or have children. When is it? They want to know, and their lingering questions mean they enter society not knowing who they are and what they are supposed to do.

This isn't a how-to book. I'm not going to give you eight steps or a checklist to complete before you declare yourself a man. Oh, if only it were that simple! Instead, as we begin our journey together, let's make sure we are asking the right questions.

I contend that manhood is not marked by any specific one-time event, but is rather a deliberate process marked by endurance, discipline, humility, repentance, service, integrity, responsibility, loyalty, commitment, and the pursuit of godliness in all things. Instead of asking yourself, *Am I a man?*, ask yourself, *Am I on the right path in my journey toward becoming a man?* This simple clarification will make all the difference.

IT'S NOT TOO LATE!

Here is your first challenge. You stand at the crossroads at this very moment. You know what is familiar and comfortable. As you continue reading, you may be unsettled as

27

you ask yourself whether you are on the right path toward true biblical manhood. However, if you stop now, you may be haunted by the wrong question, the thought, "Am I a man?" swirling about your mind for years, unresolved and unanswered.

You might be skeptical at this point. After all, I haven't told you what your journey will entail, what it will require of you, what challenges and obstacles you must overcome, and what changes it might work in you from the inside out.

However, before we set out together, allow me to share some stories that might provide a clearing in the thicket. From there, we will see a fuller picture of the path we must follow to discover our true masculine design in our journey!

DISCUSSION QUESTIONS

1. Is your life best described by the words *safety and security* or *adventure and risk*? Explain and give examples.

2. Have you ever been invited on a journey or an adventure, yet were unsure of how it would go or how it would end? Share.

3. If you have not been invited on such a journey, how would you respond to such an invitation? Would you embrace or decline the offer? Why?

4. What did it take for Peter to step out of his place of safety and security?

5. Unlike Peter, the rest of the disciples stayed in the boat. What would it take for you to leave your place of safety and embark on a journey of adventure, discovery, risk, and revelation?

REACHING HIGHER

Fears can freeze us in our tracks, unable to take the first step. Peter had been battling the wind and waves all night long, yet he stepped out in faith.

What are the winds and waves that make the first step of your own journey most unsettling? Could these fears be areas of insecurity, past mistakes, what you have been told or made to believe, overconfidence, or even the arrogant belief that you do not need to change?

- Write down your "winds and waves" on paper.
- Pray that God will give you victory over those fears.
- Share those fears with another guy.

If you do these three things, you are well on your way.

"Let us endeavor so to live that when we come to die even the undertaker will be sorry."

—*Mark Twain*[1]

TRAIL STORIES

* You have personal stories to tell that are specific and unique to you.
* The themes of your stories provide insight into your true character.
* Reflecting on your life's stories helps you assess where you are in your journey.

INTO THE EYE OF THE STORM

Seven o'clock p.m., February 5, 2008. My good friend Mark Wilson called to tell me that his son David had texted him alarming news: he and his friends had been hit by a tornado.

David Wilson had graduated from Chattanooga Christian School in Tennessee, where I am the varsity soccer coach and high school principal. Having completed a successful high school career as the soccer team captain, the student council president, and a graduate with high honors. David had accepted a soccer scholarship from Union University in Jackson, Tennessee, where he would begin studying pre-med to become a doctor.

As we discussed the situation, Mark and I knew that tornados were sweeping across Tennessee, that venturing in David's direction would be difficult and dangerous, and that David was in a bad situation.

Shortly after seven o'clock, David called his father. "Hey, I'm trapped in the bathroom of Watters Commons. I've got to call the police. I'll talk to you later."

Mark called me back, and we talked about the options. After a couple of hours, Mark decided to drive to Jackson and asked if I would make the trip with his family. We quickly met up and started what was normally a four-and-a-half hour trek to Jackson. When I called Tennessee Highway Patrol to check the status of the interstate ahead, I was greeted by a very animated state trooper who said, "Buddy, get off the road and hunker down. The interstate in Nashville is closed. It's a disaster up here!"

Thankful for GPS, we began to snake our way toward Jackson on backcountry roads. Not knowing David's status naturally made us tense and eager to arrive. Since we were driving well in excess of 100 mph, it's not surprising we were pulled over. After we explained the situation, the officer was gracious and let us go, telling us to be safe.

Here's what we didn't know at the time: David and a group of friends had gone into a basement on campus when a category F5 tornado unleashed its fury. Within seconds, the building was leveled, and David and his friends lay trapped under nineteen feet of concrete block walls and rubble.

David lay facedown in the tornado-ready position—but now with thousands of pounds of concrete on his back. After he called his father, his cell phone lost its reception, leaving him unable to contact the police. Within thirty minutes, he lost the feeling in his legs, his lungs became compressed—limiting his breathing—and the pain became almost unbearable. His friends did a roll call every fifteen minutes; some sang, some prayed, and some quoted Scripture. However, David lay in silence because finding the air even to breathe hurt his ribs.

As time wore on, hope faded. There was no relief in sight. After three hours of being pinned to the ground, David recalls praying, "Lord, if it is your will, take me home tonight, or, if it is your will, take me Home tonight." Chattanooga or heaven— either one was better than the floor of a collapsed building.

Still speeding, but still a couple of hours away, we received news at last. Mark's phone rang just before midnight, and David told him, "They're pulling me out! I'll see you at the hospital!"

Fifteen minutes before we arrived, we got a call from a friend telling Mark they had put David on a ventilator. We knew what that meant. Panic filled the car as we fervently prayed for the rest of the journey.

When we reached the hospital at two in the morning, David was alive but not doing well. We were left to pace the floor, watching the minutes slowly tick by as we awaited word from the doctors.

The early-morning reports were tough to hear. David's blood pressure had plummeted. He had respiratory failure and kidney failure. It seemed possible he would lose his legs, which had been compressed for hours. On the second day, the doctors performed a fasciectomy, a surgical procedure in which the skin is cut to relieve pressure.

For the next sixty-seven days, David experienced a roller-coaster ride of setbacks and victories. After five weeks on dialysis, his kidneys started to work properly—what a great day that was! Surgeons closed up his legs, and he began intensive therapy to start walking again. On April 11, he walked out of Siskin Rehab Hospital! Another awesome day!

Today, David will never again fly up and down the soccer field as he once did. He will not ski as he did during our stay in Snowshoe, West Virginia. Yet never—and I mean never—have

I heard David complain about what happened to him or how his life has been altered. Instead, David is quick to say God is truly the one in control of our lives: he has plans for us, and he knows what is best.

Throughout the entire incident, David has showed unparalleled character. When his story was told on national television, David was able to bear witness to God's grace and goodness, even in the eye of the storm. David has been an inspiration to many, speaking in schools, to youth groups, and in churches across the country.

While your story might not be as dramatic as David Wilson's, you will still encounter struggles along your journey. In moments of adversity, the circumstances you face will reveal your true character. May the story of David serve as a constant reminder that you can be used by God to faithfully speak of his faithfulness; may you use your testimony to encourage and benefit those around you.

While David could have turned inward and refused to share his story, he stepped out of his area of comfort much like Peter stepped out of the boat. Why? Because, like Peter, David knew Jesus would meet him at the point of his greatest need.

WHAT STORIES TELL US

When I tuck my sons in bed, the predictable request comes, "Daddy, tell us a story!" With the aim to please, I take requests. Josiah, my middle son, asks me to tell about the time I was chased by a pack of wolves. Jakob, the youngest, affirms this request. And my story begins . . .

"I was a teenager hunting in the backwoods of Vermont on a dark and snowy winter afternoon. The wind was howling; snow was sweeping across the open ground.

"Suddenly, I realized I was not alone. Just through the tree line, red, beady eyes slowly stalked my every move. The sets of eyes were growing by the minute into a full pack of wolves. Not wanting to panic, I began to walk briskly, hoping those eyes would fade into the forest once I reached the pasture. But just the opposite happened! As the pack grew in number and determination, the wolves became completely focused on me.

"As I came into the clearing, I began to jog. The wolf pack must have taken this as a sign of weakness, because they followed in hot pursuit as I sprinted toward home."

At this point in the story, my youngest interrupts to remind me that I had a gun in my hand. However, I tell him I only had four bullets left—hardly enough to take out the eight wolves chasing me. Elaborating in great detail, I tell of my realization that I couldn't outrun the wolves: I would have to take a stand and fight. My sons' eyes get as big as saucers as I tell of unloading my gun on the four closest wolves, then turning the gun around to use as a club.

Now a little nervous for his dad's sake, Jakob interrupts again. "Dad, is this true?"

"No, son, it is not!"

He shrugs his shoulder. "OK, keep going!"

When my sons ask me to tell stories, they are really asking me to tell them about life. What should they pursue? What are worthy endeavors? What is life all about? Whatever they may think about these questions, they know they want to be like their dad—despite his shortcomings.

It's true I've never fought a pack of wolves. However, I have faced other personal struggles in which I've had to decide between standing and running. While running might be the easier choice, it often leaves a sickening feeling in your gut—a feeling of incompleteness, not-knowing and not-discovering. You wonder, "What if . . . ? "

I remember when I flirted with running away during my college soccer days. The decision to stick it out made all the difference in my journey. Had I run from my problems during my sophomore year, I can't imagine how different my journey and life would be today!

STICKING IT OUT

College soccer brought me some of my best days and some of my most difficult days. Despite my rollercoaster experience, though, that time in my life may have shaped me more than any single event.

I came onto the college freshmen soccer scene thinking I was something. I started about half the games. (Not too bad for a freshman!) The summer before our sophomore season began, a new coach, Dave Murray, led a select group of college players to Holland, Belgium, Germany, and Austria. We played local teams in the towns and cities we visited.

Going into my sophomore season, I had high hopes for what the season would hold. However, Murray brought in a very strong freshmen class that bumped me from getting the playing time I thought I had earned and deserved. It was difficult for me to handle, but my coach cared enough to press me in a way I had not been pressed before. He saw me wrestling with my situation and finally came to me and said, "Shawn, you think you are better than you are. Let's sit down and watch you on tape."

Following this film review session, Murray told me what I would need to do to be a better player. It was not a fun or glamorous list and led to a long summer of mundane, arduous work. The summer between my sophomore and junior year, I took his training program and doubled whatever he asked. By the time pre-season rolled around, I was running seven miles in under forty-two minutes, and no one could beat me on timed runs. I had trained my body hard, and it paid off. By the time I was a senior, I was a starting captain and helped to lead our team to the national tournament.

Looking back, I see the process was much more important than the outcome, because that long, difficult process taught me never to quit. As Napoleon Hill wrote, "When defeat overtakes a man, the easiest and the most logical thing to do is to QUIT. That is exactly what the majority of men do."[2] I decided being like the "majority of men" was simply not acceptable, and that decision prepared me well for the rest of my life.

As I trained, I would repeat parts of the poem my coach had given me. The last few words of this poem are:

> Often the goal is nearer than it seems to a faint and
> faltering man;
> often the struggler has given up when he might have cap-
> tured the victor's cup;
> and he learned too late when the night came down,
> how close he was to the golden crown.
> . . . .
> So stick to the fight when you're hardest hit—it's when things
> seem worst, you must not quit.[3]

Because I decided not to quit, I accomplished more than I had imagined.

COMMON GOAL, UNCOMMON OUTCOME

What happens when a group of individuals holds a similar, determined mindset? What if their character and will and resolve were of one mind? What might that group be able to do if drawn together to achieve a common goal in such an uncommon manner?

I firmly believe every young man should be on a team. You might immediately think of an athletic team, but it doesn't have to be. You could join a drama team, debate team, mission team, or student council. Regardless of the type, any team will teach you valuable life lessons that will pay huge dividends in marriage, church, college, or a future occupation. Teams teach conflict resolution, collaboration, encouragement, commitment, leadership, followership, problem-solving, risk-taking, the turning of obstacles into opportunities, the proper handling of praise and criticism, the correct response to triumph or defeat, and much more. Better still, becoming a member of a Christian team allows you to view life beyond your own abilities and limitations and to see and experience the body of Christ at work.

Having coached hundreds of soccer players over the years, I have countless stories of victory and defeat I could tell. However, one story in particular leaps to the forefront of my mind.

In a fall evening in 1999, my soccer team was down 0-1 in the Florida soccer state championship final match against our longtime rival. With only several minutes remaining, I began to push all our players forward as we desperately made every possible attempt to secure the equalizing goal. Seeing what we were doing, the opposition began to drive balls off the sideline, probably intending to knock the balls far away so we wouldn't have one to throw in.

As the crowd began to chant, "Ten, nine, eight, seven—", they were interrupted by the official's whistle to stop the clock. The official had noticed that while there was still some time left on the clock, the ball had been played far away from the playing field and no ball was available for a quick restart. This gave us a couple seconds to set up one last desperate attempt.

Even our best strategizing could not have predicted what happened next. The clock began again. The opposing team's fans picked up where they had left off. "Seven, six, five, four, three—"

But the announcer interrupted them with the yell of "GOOOOAAAAAL!"

The play that had unfolded in those five seconds was beyond words. As Alex hurled the ball toward the box, Jason rose above the defenders and flicked the ball backward. The keeper was dashing to punch the ball away. Before he could get to it, Ryan flicked the ball again. Just before the ball hit the ground, our left midfielder, Matt, came sprinting across the goal box and hit a full volley into the back of the net. The ball never touched the ground until it crossed the goal line.

How quickly the tide had turned! Stunned, the opposing players dropped to the ground. That dramatic goal filled our young men with such indescribable excitement and energy. A few seconds before, we had been devastated. Now we were on top of the world.

When the overtime whistle blew, we knew who would come out on top. Five minutes into overtime, Brandon rifled a twenty-five yard blast into the opposite upper corner for the go-ahead-goal! When the final whistle blew, our team experienced every emotion as we laughed and cried and enjoyed a moment no one could take from us.

You need to know that many of those players had been together for many years. I had coached them back when they were in fifth and sixth grade. They knew each other. They knew hard work. They had set a goal, knowing an uncommon outcome was possible as long as time remained on the clock.

STORIES OF YOUR OWN

As you have read these stories, I hope your mind has filled with stories of your own. Even if you can't think of some right this minute, you do indeed have stories to tell. Consider how they have shaped you. What do they say about you? What have they revealed in you? Where might they take you?

Your stories are a part of your journey. They show you where you've been, and they show you where you're going. While they're useful to you, they are also worth sharing.

In 2007, I helped to lead the senior class on a three-day retreat. Prior to our final session, a senior named Brad Gibson asked if he could share what God had done in his life over the previous six months. Brad took this step without knowing how he would be perceived or how his classmates would respond to him. He had the passion and conviction to tell his story.

And he did just that! After the closing talk by our keynote speaker, Brad openly proclaimed how God had rescued and redeemed him. Occasionally fighting back tears, he explained he was in love with Jesus Christ and had decided to live for him and no longer for himself.

No one expected what followed. After listening to Brad, Anselmo "Mo" Heath courageously rose and shared how Jesus had invaded his heart and how he would never go back to his former ways. He was quickly followed by Ben Sandidge and many other fellow students who stood and shared of their hurt and pain and struggles, openly confessing their sins. Many others turned their lives over to Christ that very night.

When the seniors returned to campus, they returned a changed class. For the next few weeks, other students followed their lead and stood in front of the entire high school student body to give testimony and glory to God's work in their lives. Before long, well over a hundred middle and high school students had submitted their lives to Christ for the first time or else recommitted their lives to Jesus Christ as their Lord and Savior.

Brad, Mo, and Ben are now juniors in college. When we occasionally get together for coffee or lunch, I have the opportunity to hear how God is working in their lives and how they are being used by God to bless those around them.

Your stories are important whether they describe your triumphs or your struggles. Have you considered telling them to others? Have you considered living in a way that will give you good stories to tell? God called Brad, Mo, and Ben out of their comfort zones to give their testimony, and he strengthened them for that task. He will equip you as well, so you need not worry about the outcome.

ARE YOU READY?

I've shared some stories from my own journey. Now it's time for you to begin yours. As Sam told Frodo at the start of their journey in The Lord of the Rings, "Remember what Bilbo used to say: 'It's a dangerous business, Frodo, going out your door. You step onto the road, and if you don't keep your feet, there's no knowing where you might be swept off to.' "[4]

As you reflect on your life thus far, identify the top three to five stories that define who you are today. These may cast a good or a not-so-good light on your life. The reality is that they each say something about who you are and the journey you have been on. I cannot promise that this will be an easy task, but you must not skip over this important process. A clear understanding of the past will provide clarity for the present and assist in making the future worth pursuing.

DISCUSSION QUESTIONS

Your stories tell a great deal about you. The ones I've told in this chapter are marked by adventure, discovery, risk, and self-revelation. Their themes are perseverance, courage, service, and teamwork.

Now the time has come for you to share your own personal and unique stories.

1. What are the elements of adventure and risk in your stories? What are some themes? Explain.

2. What did you learn about yourself through these adventures?

3. In telling these stories, have you gained new revelations about yourself? (Consider: Did you choose risk or safety? Did you follow or lead? Were you courageous or timid? Did you work with a team or as an individual? Did you engage in the action or were you a spectator?)

4. If you had the chance to participate in your adventure(s) again, would you? If not, why not? If yes, is there anything you might do or say differently?

5. What are the stories that are integral to your life's past and present journey, but which you do not want anyone to know? Why are these difficult to share? Do they hinder forward progress in your journey? (If these questions are difficult for you, it is my hope that through our journey together over the next 14 chapters, you will know and believe that your past and present are redeemed in and through the blood of Christ and that you *can* venture on this journey toward biblical manhood.)

REACHING HIGHER

As you reflect on this chapter and your answers to the questions above, describe how you would summarize your character at this point in your journey. Are you pleased by what you see? If not pleased, then identify what character challenges you'll need to address if presented with a similar test of character.

PART 2

THE JOURNEY BEGINS

"What is a man? Does anyone know?
TELL ME!
Who is the prototype? To whom shall I go?"

—*unnamed young man, as quoted by Robert Lewis*[1]

THE TRAIL GUIDE

GUIDEPOSTS

* The men who guide and mentor you play a vital, pivotal role in your journey.
* The stories and life experiences of older men will help you as you navigate toward manhood.
* A healthy mentoring relationship must be founded on trust.

"GUYS, GIVE ME YOUR FLASHLIGHTS. I'm going on ahead. As a team, work together to press on and find me."

My college soccer team was deep below the earth's surface in the heart of West Virginia's caves, so those were not necessarily the words we wanted to hear from our coach. But with very little notice, he gathered our flashlights, leaving us to fumble our way toward him in pitch darkness.

Up to that point, we had squeezed through cracks and crevices, doing army crawls through muddy tunnels barely large enough for our biggest guys to fit through. For the most part, we had had good attitudes about it all. However, this new predicament was a huge challenge, especially for our goalkeeper. On a normal day, he never shut his mouth. However, we had discovered he was claustrophobic and the tight spaces were just about too much for him. For the next five hours, he was almost completely silent.

When our coach's light disappeared, we realized he had left us to our own devices. We began to strategize the best way to proceed. After much arguing, we finally appointed leaders to get us to our coach. For the next twenty minutes, we blindly felt our way through the tunnels. Guys began to call out the obstacles they had encountered before the rest of us could stumble and trip over them. It didn't ultimately matter who was in the lead; this was a case of the blind leading the blind.

After what seemed like eternity, the guy in the front of the line yelled, "I found Coach!"

Our coach stood up and shone his flashlight back the way we had come. To our astonishment, we had walked less than fifty feet.

While I could draw out many life lessons from this experience, the primary lesson I learned was that without our guide, we wouldn't have made it out of those underground tunnels— at least, not for a long, long time. Coach Murray had spent many weekends in the caves, and the time he had logged had brought him great experience. He didn't need maps because he was familiar with each tunnel. He had undoubtedly made mistakes and learned lessons, making him capable of leading an entire team through an underground maze. Seeing this, we quickly learned to trust him as our guide.

As I've raised my three sons, I've watched with interest as they've developed this type of trust. At times, they have made the greatest strides through costly lessons. For example, I have told each of them not to touch the hot stovetop. Without fail, each one has reached up to the stove and burned his hand. Panicking and confused, each has exclaimed, "Ahhhh, that's hot! I just burned my hand, Daddy!" Unfortunately, some lessons are learned the hard way. Lack of the necessary trust plus a generous portion of curiosity prove a poor combination.

As soccer players in a cave, we were in a very unfamiliar setting. Low risk and high trust seemed the best way to go. At one point, Coach Murray led us through a winding tunnel that opened into a cavern. He warned us to resist the urge to stand upright the second we entered the open space. When we asked him why, he simply said, "Trust me!"

One by one, we made our way into the cavern. It immediately became clear why Coach had given us those instructions. Shining our flashlights on the cave ceiling, we saw hundreds and hundreds of bats hanging upside-down sleeping, literally inches from our heads.

I have often wondered what would have happened if one of us had stood up, bumped some bats, and wakened them from their sleep. I'm sure pandemonium would have exploded. As we left that cave, we were glad to a man that each player had taken Coach at his word that day. It was just one of the experiences that caused me to consider my coach a trustworthy and reliable trail guide.

YOU NEED A TRAIL GUIDE

I have watched my three sons go through a transitional stage in their lives. Until the age of four or five, my wife was the center of their universe. For them, her love, nurture, care, and compassion were everything. In fact, my youngest son, Jakob, told me almost nightly, "Mom is my favorite" or "Only Mom can snuggle at bedtime."

As they have grown, my sons have retained their deep love for their mother and greatly appreciate all she has done for them and instilled in them. At the same time, they have begun to look to me as their father more and more for guidance, direction, and a vision for whom they should be. My wife and I never told our sons to shift their attention from their mother to me. We never instructed them to watch and learn and emulate what I do to figure out who they are to become. The transition occurred naturally. Mom is still very important to them, but I am the one they want to imitate.

Why is this important? By purposefully watching and learning, my sons are developing a sense of their true masculine design and identity and a sense of belonging. They are learning what they should value in life, what type of character they should exhibit, what true love looks like, and how they can show respect to others (particularly women). Since I'm a sinner, it's also good for my sons to see how I respond when I make mistakes.

However, I'm not the only one they should be watching! It didn't take long for my sons to see that Dad also has areas of needed growth. I love my sons and deeply value our relationships, which means there is a relationship I desire for them that is far more important than their relationship with me. Humanly speaking, that is hard to say, but it is the truth!

God our Father desires to have an intimate relationship with us. He reveals himself to us through the reading of his word. The more we read of him, the more we learn about ourselves since he is the one in whose image, character, and design we are fashioned. The more we learn of our Father, the more we start to resemble him in speech, character, and conduct. He is a relational God who is near to us (Ps. 145:18), who will help us when we don't know what we ought to pray (Rom. 8:26), and who will generously give us wisdom when we ask him for it (James 1:5).

As well as our earthly father and our heavenly one, other men share themselves with us in ways that make the gospel message clearer. As we watch them, we catch a glimpse of God's truth playing out in their lives.

In 1 Thessalonians 2:8, Paul tells the church of Thessalonica, "We loved you so much that we were delighted to share with you not only the gospel of God but our lives as well, because you had become so dear to us." This pivotal verse connects the gospel *and* godly men. The gospel and the role of other men in leading and mentoring you complement one another instead of coming into conflict. They go hand in hand. Therefore, I suggest every young man have an older, experienced man come alongside him to point the way and help him navigate the difficult and dark places of life.

WHY DO YOU NEED ANYBODY?

This idea might sound ridiculous. You may be thinking, "Hey, wait a minute! As I near adulthood, I should experience *more* freedom, *more* independence, and the opportunity to make *more* decisions on my own. I've been listening to others tell me what to do all my life. Now it's my time."

If you feel threatened by allowing someone else to speak into your life, then ask yourself, "Why do I feel this way? Why do I get tense and defensive at this thought? What are these emotions and impulses telling me about my heart?"

If you never ask these questions and meditate on them, you will never find important heart-level answers. I challenge you to consider the words of Larry Crabb, who writes,

> Men are easily threatened. And whenever a man is threatened, when he becomes uncomfortable in places within himself that he does not understand, he naturally retreats into an arena of comfort or competence, or he dominates someone or something in order to feel powerful. . . . As a result, most men feel close to no one, especially not to God, and no one feels close to them.
>
> Something good in men is stopped and needs to get moving. When good movement stops, bad movement (retreat or domination) reliably develops.[2]

If you feel defensive or uncomfortable at the thought of letting another man lead you into the unknown, those feelings further reveal your character. Your heart is understandable. We all want to believe we have it all together and don't need anyone. Yet if we achieve our desire for autonomy, self-reliance, and independence from support, advice, accountability, and correction, we become like the first man, who was cut off from an intimate relationship with God.

Imagine what Adam went through. The first night after he was exiled from Eden, how he must have longed to walk again with God in the cool of the evening. When Eve was birthing Cain, how Adam must have desired a word of advice from God on how to ease his wife's pain, the result of his sin. How Adam must have longed for divine encouragement when his firstborn son killed his brother in cold blood. Over Adam's 930 years on this earth, how he must have thought regularly of paradise and deeply regretted the day he had rejected God, thinking he no longer needed him. How dearly we all have paid for his arrogant, self-centered decision.

In your journey, you will be confronted with situations where you will desperately need the help of another man. At times, you will question whether you have what it takes to get through not just the day but the very next moment! If you have not been seeking wisdom and counsel from a man who has learned from past mistakes or from his own mentors and personal walk with the Lord, you may take a hard fall on your journey. Willingness to let another man speak into your life requires humility and the recognition that you *don't* have it all together and that you *do* need help. There is no disgrace, there is no loss of honor, and you are no less of a man when you admit you need help.

The Scriptures tell us that God resists the proud but gives grace to the humble (cf. Prov. 3:34). J. C. Ryle called pride "the oldest sin in the world" and wrote that "pride stocked hell with its first inhabitants."[3] Pride ultimately puts young men in very dangerous positions.

Look at how God speaks into the matter:

> When pride comes, then comes disgrace,
>   but with humility comes wisdom. (Prov. 11:2)

> Pride goes before destruction,
>   a haughty spirit before a fall. (Prov. 16:18)

> A man's pride brings him low,
>   but a man of lowly spirit gains honor. (Prov. 29:23)

Notice the words associated with pride (disgrace, low, destruction, fall) versus words associated with humility (wisdom and honor).

FINDING AND LEARNING

It is vitally important that godly men speak into your life and your heart. The way can be steep and rough, and you will need guidance and direction. Youth groups, small groups, accountability partners, and retreats can powerfully change lives. However, true biblical masculinity must be sought and found in something deeper and more personal than programs.

For years, I have prayed that God would provide other godly men who might speak into my sons' lives, whether they be teachers, youth workers, coaches, etc. I thank God that already my thirteen-year-old son has several key mentors. As well as his dad, he has a soccer coach who loves the Lord. This coach views athletics as a way to maximize our God-given gifts and use them as an act of worship while fiercely battling on the field. From this starting position, he challenges my son, pushes him, exhorts him, holds him accountable, and loves him deeply through every step of his journey as if he were his very own son.

In the indescribable providence of God, my son's current youth group leader was the central defender for the team we defeated in the previous chapter. That game took place in Florida. We lived an hour away from each other and did not know one another except as names on a roster sheet. Unbeknownst to each other, we both moved to Lookout Mountain, Georgia. Eleven years ago, when I was simultaneously praying that God would lead other Christian men into my son's life and that the Lord would give us victory in the 1999 state championship over our opponent, little did I know that both my prayers concerned the very same man whom God is using to impact my own son's life! How mysterious and awesome is our God!

WITHSTANDING HEART ATTACKS

Note that I am discussing *biblical* masculinity, for to be truly manly, one must be godly. This simple qualifier changes everything. Without it, masculinity is reduced to possessing big trucks and fast cars, dating beautiful women, and strutting around with a Herculean physique. Unless we look at masculinity from a biblical perspective, we deal only with external matters instead of examining issues of the heart. But getting to the heart is very difficult. In order to truly know each other and ourselves, we must go to the Scriptures, which say, "Above all else, guard your heart, for it is the wellspring of life" (Prov. 4:23).

If you want to be known truly, you must reveal your heart. King David, a man after God's own heart, made the most vulnerable request when he asked God to search his heart, to know him and to try him, to see if there was any wicked way in him, and to lead him in the way everlasting (cf. Ps. 139)!

Why would King David take his most valuable possession, his heart, and leave it so completely defenseless? He wanted to be deeply and intimately known by God. He knew the darkness of his own heart. He knew its propensity to rebel against God. He knew he needed to be held accountable and to be led as he in turn led the Kingdom of Israel.

My senior pastor, Joe Novenson, one of the most humble men I know, regularly makes his elders a similar petition: "My heart is an open hunting ground. If you see something there that is not right, have at it!" How unnerving, how naked and transparent!

The thought of speaking this way would paralyze most men, since we rarely have conversations that reach the heart level! If you don't believe me, watch what men do when they get together in a group. During our initial handshakes and greetings, we size each other up by declaring what we do. If we feel inadequate because our counterpart holds a more highly esteemed occupation, we namedrop and sneak references to our many accomplishments into the conversation. All the while, we make mental judgment calls about whether the people we are conversing with are worthy of our time and attention. If we are groping for respect out of the fear that we're not measuring up, we resort to talking about the glory days of high school football or to rattling off the scores and statistics of recent games. A pervasive shallowness defines these conversations and relationships. In the end, men walk away feeling just as empty and unconnected as they did prior to the conversation.

Having spoken to large crowds, taught a number of classes, and coached a variety of teams (listing my credentials here), I have learned that nothing comes close to the one-on-one, life-on-life relationships the Lord has allowed me to have with students and athletes over the years. We need men who will declare to younger men, "It can be done. I have done what you are attempting to do. You are not alone. I will walk with you because I believe in you!"

I wish I could promise that a specific man in your life will come alongside you as your trail guide and older brother. I simply can't do that. But I do propose that you prepare yourself to be led. Watch and pray and see whom God might bring into your life.

Some of you might find the boldness and the courage to pursue a trail guide or mentor now. Look at the example of Elijah and Elisha's mentoring relationship in the Scriptures. In Elisha's day, this process took place as "the two of them walked on" (2 Kings 2:6). When Elijah tried to leave Elisha, Elisha would not let him. His vow—"As surely as the Lord lives and as you live, I will not leave you" (2 Kings 2:2)—embodies his resolve to pursue and remain with Elijah.

Although many books are written on mentoring, I will mention one particularly important quality for your mentor to have. Observe how he responds to the sin in his life. This will tell you a great deal about him and about how he might best serve you. Instead of deflecting guilt, shifting blame, and making excuses, this person should fully and humbly depend on God and pursue a growing relationship with him. His life should be marked by a brokenness and a repentance over his sin. You can expect him to be a sinner. What he does with that sin is of utmost importance. The right response reveals his relationship with God and his ability to lead you toward true biblical masculinity.

As you prepare to be led, consider these few important prerequisites for a mentoring relationship. You may need to wrestle with these before beginning your journey.

A Teachable Spirit

Dangers and pitfalls fill the way. If you are not willing to hear and respond appropriately to suggestions, instructions, or requirements, the journey may become even more hazardous. As C. S. Lewis wrote, "Experience is a brutal teacher, but you learn."[4] Your trail guide, like my college coach, has gone before and has made costly mistakes and learned valuable life lessons. These lessons will be great gifts for you if you listen, learn, and respond to them. Instead of making similar costly errors, you will walk in truth and in light.

Willingness to Trust

If your life is marked by one broken promise after another, learning to trust will be difficult. However, over time, trust can develop! In fact, it *must* develop in order for authentic, heart-level conversations to occur. Henri Nowen said,

> To wait open-endedly is an enormously radical attitude toward life. So is to trust that something will happen to us that is far beyond our own imaginings. So, too, is giving up control over our future and letting God define our life, trusting that God molds us according to God's love and not according to our fear. The spiritual life is a life in which we [wait] actively present to the moment, trusting that new things will happen to us, new things that are far beyond our own imagination, fantasy, or prediction. That, indeed, is a very radical stance toward life in a world preoccupied with control.[5]

Appetite for Adventure

Along the way, you may be asked to attempt something that drives you from your comfort zone. You can approach this as an inconvenience and obstacle or as an adventure and opportunity. In *My Utmost for His Highest*, Oswald Chambers describes the latter perspective this way: "To be certain of God means that we are uncertain in all our ways, we do not know what day may bring forth. This is generally said with a sigh of sadness; it should rather be an expression of breathless expectation. . . . When we are rightly related to God, life is full of spontaneous, joyful uncertainty and expectancy."[6]

Openness to Change

I once heard it said: "There are few people that like change in life. While a baby may like a changed diaper, even then he cries!" The most difficult change takes place in our hearts. Author William Gurnall wrote, "God would not rub so hard if it were not to fetch out the dirt that is ingrained in our natures. God loves purity so well He had rather see a hole than a spot in His child's garments."[7]

Perseverance!

Even after he received a blow that made him lame, Jacob would not give up wrestling with God until he had obtained the blessing (cf. Gen. 32:25–26). In the same way, you will experience setbacks and discouragements. Hold on, stay on the path, and press on!

DISCUSSION QUESTIONS

1. Have you ever relied on another person's experience or expertise to get you through a difficult situation? Explain.

2. During such experiences, what was required from you?

3. What thoughts or emotions rise when you think of another person guiding you through the ups and downs of life?

4. Your experiences with your father or other significant men in your life will cause you to embrace or repel the leadership and guidance of other men. Are you willing or reluctant to have a life-mentor (one who is older and a bit more seasoned with life experiences) lead and speak truth into your life? Explain your answer.

5. Of the five personal prerequisites needed by you in a healthy mentoring relationship, which of these comes most naturally and which will require the most focus, attention, and prayer? Discuss.

REACHING HIGHER

Make a list of men whose character and integrity you admire and whom you would like to have as trail guides to assist in leading you in your journey toward manhood. A bold step would be to ask one of them to lead you in that capacity.

It would be helpful for you to tell that man where you are in the prerequisites you need for a healthy mentoring relationship.

"We few, we happy few, we band of brother[s];
For he to-day that sheds his blood with me
Shall be my brother; be he ne'er so vile
This day shall gentle his condition:
And gentlemen in England, now a-bed
Shall think themselves accurs'd they were not here,
And hold their manhoods cheap whiles any speaks
That fought with us upon Saint Crispin's day."

—*William Shakespeare*[1]

JOINED BY A BAND OF BROTHERS

GUIDEPOSTS

* ✳ Men need other men in their lives.
* ✳ Life can beat you and pin you to the ground. Who will pick you up?
* ✳ True friends stick with you even when it is not convenient or advantageous.
* ✳ True friendships are marked by an uncommon bond, love, loyalty, and full disclosure.

LET'S FACE IT: most guy relationships are fairly shallow. We hang out and talk about the things we have in common and enjoy doing together. We listen to music, watch movies, watch games, play on the same team, go hunting, go fishing, go rock-climbing, go golfing, go camping, and on and on. For the most part, our relationships are defined by the activities we have in common. As a result, we thoroughly enjoy sitting around a campfire, reminiscing about the good ol' days as we tell stories that always begin "Do you remember when . . . ?" (For me, the stories go like this, "Hey, Brower, do you remember that time you jumped off that platform on the high ropes course and almost died?" or "Remember when we snuck into coach's house while he was there, swiped his car keys, took the tires off his Bronco, and put it on cinder blocks?")

FRIENDS BECOME ALLIES

Without a doubt, life is an adventure. As we journey on, we'll enjoy the adventure even more when we're joined by those who have the same interests, men we can slap on the back for a job well done or laugh and celebrate with.

Yet, in the ebb and flow of our adventures in life, we run into battles and travel through valleys, facing trials and adversities that are almost too much to bear alone. In such moments, the strength that allowed us to climb mountains, swim oceans, conquer fears, and brave the elements now isolates us from others. We are shaken to the core and too embarrassed to admit we need help. After all, a man's strength is his identity; it is what makes a man a man.

Let's call this response for what it is: pride. Yet more than pride is involved. We also feel awkward when we even consider approaching one of our buddies to let him know we need help. Why? Because such conversations rarely, if ever, happen. Patrick Morley, author of *The Man in the Mirror* and father of one of the many soccer players who has played for me over the years, observes that while most men could recruit six pallbearers, "hardly anyone has a friend he can call at 2:00 AM."[2]

Expecting to maneuver through life unscathed is simply naïve. Not only does life test your strength, but also your character, principles, morals, and ultimately your relationships. When we waver, stumble, or fall, we need brothers who will not only bear us up, but who will also be willing to speak the truth and say it like it is—call a spade a spade.

These brothers are more than accountability partners who seek to keep you on a good path. Instead, they are fellow soldiers in the foxhole next to yours. You depend on them for your life.

In the 2001 TV series, *Band of Brothers*, solider Bill Guarnere says, "Once we get into combat, the only people you can trust is yourself and the fella next to you."[3] In war, the meaning of trust is ramped up to an entirely different level: it means willingly putting your life into another man's hands. Soldiers who want to get through the war zone alive have to watch each other's backs. They are bound to get hit at some point and when that happens, they will need each other to bind wounds and possibly to shoulder each other to safety. Another character in *Band of Brothers* says, "Don't worry, there's so much crap flying around, you're bound to get dinged sometime. Almost every one of these guys got hit at least once."[4]

In other words, wounds are expected.

FRIENDS IN ACTION

On November 16, 2010, Staff Sergeant Salvatore "Sal" A. Giunta received our nation's highest military decoration, the Medal of Honor. It was the first time in forty years that the medal had been extended to a living person. Sal had served two tours of duty in Afghanistan. During his first tour, his team leader had told him, "You just try—you just got to try to do everything you can when it's your time to do it."[5] Sal did that and more!

While patrolling in northern Afghanistan, Sal and his men walked into an ambush. The enemy pounded their location with hundreds of rounds of bullets. With three men fallen, Sal raced through the gunfire to drag an injured comrade to safety, ignoring a hit to his body armor and another to the weapon he carried.

Both sides exchanged intense fire as Sal and his company charged headlong into the hail of bullets to rescue a comrade shot twice in the leg and unable to move. Sal then dashed over the top of the hill in time to see another friend—one of his best friends—being dragged away by two of the enemy. Sal didn't hesitate. He killed the first man, injured the second, and dragged his wounded friend to cover. For the next half-hour, he worked to stabilize his condition until help arrived.

Before awarding Sal the medal, President Barack Obama said:

> "Staff Sergeant Giunta, repeatedly and without hesitation . . . charged forward through extreme enemy fire, embodying the warrior ethos that says, "I will never leave a fallen comrade." . . . That's why Salvatore Giunta risked his life for his fellow soldiers—because they would risk their lives for him. That's what fueled his bravery—not just the urgent impulse to have their backs, but the absolute confidence that they had his. One of them, Sal has said—of these young men that he was with, he said, "They are just as much of me as I am." [6]

On receiving the medal, Sal said, "Although this is so positive, I would give this back in a second to have my friends with me right now." [7]

BE PREPARED

Maybe you have not served nor have any plans to serve in the military. That does not mean this chapter does not apply to you. Not one of us is exempt from the inevitable winds and waves that smash into our lives.

In Matthew 7:24–27, Jesus tells a story of the wise man, who builds his house on a rock, and the foolish man, who builds his house on the sand. In each case, Jesus says, "The rain came down, the streams rose, and the winds blew and beat against that house." Regardless of how you build your life, regardless of the foundation you have established, the winds and the waves of life will crash down on you in some form or another.

Is it possible to survive those times on your own? Perhaps. However, a band of brothers marked by full disclosure and transparency can ease each other's pain, bear each other's burdens, and make life's setbacks and struggles bearable. In chapter 2, I spoke of David Wilson, trapped under nineteen feet of rubble. Instead of complaining or panicking, his friends' response was to sing to their God and King, to call Scripture to mind, and to pray to the One who controls the winds and waves and F5 tornadoes. Though pinned to the floor of that building, they stood tall on the immovable Rock! One of David's close friends had a free hand, which he used to pull the hood off David's head to reduce the sweltering heat. During the hours they were trapped, he held David's hand as they battled through the experience together.

Sometimes guys whom I have coached or taught over the years call or text me and say, "Hey, we've got to do lunch or get breakfast soon. I need to tell you what's going on in my life. I need some advice." I absolutely love to get those contacts. Just the other day, I got one from a former student whom I had not seen in over eight years. Over lunch, we spent a great deal of time reminiscing about his graduating class and talking about his church life, his new bride, and so on.

I have strong relationships with the soccer players I coach. They call me Coach, sometimes think of me as a mentor, or even see something in me that they want to emulate in their own lives. However, I am not their friend in the true sense of the word. Don't get me wrong—I have stood as a groomsman at their weddings and by their bedsides when doctors thought they were dying; I have celebrated the birth of their firstborns and stood at one's funeral. I love my players like my sons, yet our relationship is a mentoring one. While these friendships are important and even vital, I want you to pursue a "band of brothers" that will mutually care for, encourage, exhort, commend, and admonish each other, that will be loyal and completely committed.

BORN FOR ADVERSITY

Solomon says in Proverbs 17:17:

A friend loves at all times,
and a brother is born for adversity.

In Ecclesiastes 4:9–10, the author writes,

Two are better than one,
    because they have a good return for their work:
If one falls down,
    his friends can help him up.
But pity the man who falls
    and has no one to help him up!

At all times, in all places, and in every way, men need brothers to stand side by side and come through for each other time after time in whatever way might be required. Henri Nowen writes, "The friend who can be silent with us in a moment of despair or confusion, who can stay with us in an hour of grief and bereavement, who can tolerate not knowing . . . not healing, not curing . . . that is a friend who cares."[8] At times, you can offer nothing more than your presence and your silence.

At some point, however, words must be spoken. You can find anyone to offer advice, but what type of advice will he give you? In the Bible, we read about a man named Job who was blessed with much. About the only thing he was not blessed with was good counsel from others. God allowed Satan to test Job to see if he would turn his back on God if his life were brought low. After his ten children suddenly died and his wealth and possessions were reduced to nothing, Job was left with a wife who told him to curse God and die and three friends who essentially said all his misery was the result of a serious sin in his life.

You must have friends who are firmly grounded on the Rock of Ages, who can offer sound, wise biblical advice to help you persevere through the difficulties of life. Psalm 1:1–4 gives us a clear picture of what this looks like:

> Blessed is the man
>   who does not walk in the counsel of the wicked
> or stand in the way of sinners
>   or sit in the seat of mockers.
> But his delight is in the law of the Lord,
>   and on his law he meditates day and night.
> He is like a tree planted by streams of water
>   which yields its fruit in season
> and whose leaf does not wither.
>   Whatever he does prospers.

A friend committed both to you and to God's word will be able to help you to navigate through the difficulties of life.

"The best way out is the way through," wrote the poet Robert Frost.[9] Too often, in our male conquering mode, we want to solve the problem the quickest and easiest way. We like to live a life of avoidance, either pretending nothing is wrong or addressing the symptoms without going after the real issue. Unfortunately, life deals you blows—some self-inflicted—that take much time, energy, and emotion to properly address. You will need friends who can keep you on the path when everything about you wants to take the easy way out.

Over the years, I have seen young men get young women pregnant out of wedlock, or get in trouble with the law, or fail out of the first year of college because they just wanted to have a good time. Others fall out of grace with their parents, typically due to mistakes they have made, until they are not welcome at home any longer. These "life-changers" rock your world. At such times, it seems like everyone is looking but no one is helping. Your true friendships will be tested and revealed in those moments.

True friendship is not about convenience, good feelings, or the benefits you can get from it. Instead, true friendship means being there despite inconvenience, standing alongside when your first reaction is "I don't have the time," or helping when even an association with the person or issue does not put you in the best light. A true friend has a responsibility to "rejoice with those who rejoice, weep with those who weep" (Rom. 12:15 ESV). When you hurt, I hurt; when you win, I win; when tragedy strikes you, it also strikes me. True friendship is walking through the pain of life, softening blows by absorbing some of their effects whenever possible. When I have been hurting or when I have failed, my closest friends have inevitably come through and been there for me in some of life's most trying moments.

THE FRIEND BY YOUR SIDE

In 1947, Jackie Robinson broke the color barrier in baseball by becoming the first African-American to play in the major leagues. In his first season with the Brooklyn Dodgers, he had fastballs thrown at his head and racial slurs shouted at him from the stands and the opposing dugouts. He was threatened and attacked.

During one game in Cincinnati, the taunts and curses of the crowd were almost too much for one man to handle. Another Dodger, shortstop Pee Wee Reese, called a time-out. He walked from shortstop to first base and put his arm around Robinson's shoulder. This single act of compassion silenced the crowd.[10]

Real men stand together, real men need each other, and real men love each other! Hal Moore and Joe Galloway capture this type of brotherly love in their book about the Vietnam War, *We Were Soldiers Once . . . and Young*:

> We discovered in that depressing, hellish place, where death was our constant companion, that we loved each other. We killed for each other, we died for each other, and we wept for each other. And in time we came to love each other as brothers. In battle our world shrank to the man on our left and the man on our right and the enemy all around. We held each other's lives in our hands and we learned to share fears, our hopes, our dreams as readily as we shared what little else good came our way.[11]

Do you have a band of brothers that will stand beside you when the bullets are flying about you, when you want to throw in the towel, or when you can't believe what life has just handed you? You need friends who will throw their arms around you as if to say, "It will be all right. We are going to do this thing together!"

A friend from my own band of brothers recently learned his wife of two years was pregnant. Within a few short weeks, the overwhelming joy of this news turned to grief when she had a miscarriage. Several weeks afterward, he went on his annual camping/backpacking trip with his five closest brothers from high school. When he returned, I asked him about his time with them. "It could not have come at a better time," he said, and I could see it in his face. He had needed to go into the wild with his closest friends and have them speak words of comfort, hope, and encouragement to him.

It is important that you know my friend is thirty-two years old. Those relationships he developed in high school were deep, significant, and necessary . . . to the point where his friends set aside time each year to intentionally get away to catch up and speak truth into each other's lives.

These types of friendships are rare. They don't just happen. Instead, you must intentionally pursue your band of brothers. Don't wait until a crisis hits. Find non-emotional reasons to get together. Your life doesn't have to be in shambles for you to have a serious talk. Invest in each other during the good times. That way, when the blows of life knock you off your feet, you will know where you can go . . . and for that, you will forever be grateful.

THE HAPPY FEW

Many years from now, may you look back and say like Staff Sergeant Salvatore A. Giunta that you did everything you could for your band of brothers when your time came. They will need your help as much as you need theirs. Don't stand idly by as your brothers are taken out left and right. Be men of action! Someday, you may speak words similar to this German general's speech at the end of *Band of Brothers*:

> Men, it's been a long war, it's been a tough war. You've fought bravely, proudly for your country. You're a special group. You've found in one another a bond that exists only in combat among brothers. You've shared foxholes,

held each other in dire moments. You've seen death and suffered together. I'm proud to have served with each and every one of you.[12]

Below are four characteristics that define such an uncommon brotherhood. Evaluate your friendships today. What needs to change or develop to make them stronger?

Uncommon Bond

An uncommon bond that will unite you and your friends for life must be rooted in similar values. It makes sense for my friends and me to be bound together since we love the same God, have the same passions, hold many of the same hopes and dreams, tread similar paths in life, become impassioned about the same injustices, have a similar vision for our families and for our sons, and have many of the same ideas for what we believe life in the Kingdom of God can and should be. Now, it's not necessary for you to have the same interests or the same life pursuits as your friends, but your values must be in sync. How do you know what those values are? You learn by having many, many deep conversations about life.

Every Monday, I lead a group of senior guys in a weekly study. We determined right away not to spend the time talking about games from the past weekend or about up-and-coming events. These guys have known each other for many years and can have those conversations outside our group time. Instead, we decided to focus on God's word and on deepening relationships through the discussions that rise from the Scripture and topic for the day.

It has been amazing to hear them speak of fears, anxieties, sin in their lives, and the difficult struggles they are encountering. I have been greatly encouraged to see them bear each other up, offering words of encouragement and empathy and challenging each other to press toward a new day and a new beginning.

An uncommon bond stems from shared values. Find those values, pursue them, and talk about them—for they will bind you together for a lifetime.

Uncommon Love

Scripture provides a powerful example of uncommon love in the relationship between David and Jonathan.[13] After David killed Goliath,

> Jonathan became one in spirit with David, and he loved him as himself. . . . And Jonathan made a covenant with David because he loved him as himself. Jonathan took off the robe he was wearing and gave it to David, along with his tunic, and even his sword, his bow and his belt. (1 Sam. 18:1, 3–4)

How powerful was their love? Jonathan essentially signed over to David his every right and privilege to the throne. By his actions, he was saying, "What is mine is yours. Take all of it." In a world powered by the drive for prestige and position, is this not jaw-dropping love and affection?

Notice what is not present. There is no jealousy, no envy, no comparison, no measuring up, and no positioning. In the world's eyes, Jonathan had every right to be jealous of the battle hero. Instead, his strongest desire was for a deep friendship with David!

True friends draw strength from each other and each other's accomplishments. In this way, they show an uncommon love.

Uncommon Loyalty

Have you ever been in a group of people where one of your friends is being run down? How did you respond? Did you stand up for him despite the potential consequences? Are you the same toward your band of brothers whether present or absent?

In 1 Samuel 19:1–5, we see King Saul wanting to put David to death out of jealousy. In fact, he tells his son Jonathan and all his servants to kill David. But Jonathan boldly steps up to the king and speaks on David's behalf. In essence, he says, "Hey, if anyone should be jealous here, I'm the one. After all, I'm the prince, the heir to the throne. However, I love this guy. Can't you see that he is one of us? He's a good guy. Look at all he has done for the children of Israel!"

Jonathan doesn't stop there. He runs to David and informs him of his father's plot to kill him.

These two men knew something bad would happen to one of them in their lifetime. Jonathan was a prince who could never take the throne, and David was being pursued by a king who wanted him dead. Could their friendship endure? Could it stand the test of such conflict?

First Samuel 20:17 reads, "And Jonathan had David reaffirm his oath out of love for him, because he loved him as he loved himself." What was this oath? The oath was "If you die, I will care for your children so your family name will endure." Are you sensing the intensity of these brothers' conversations?

Over the years, I have had a couple brothers ask me, "If something were to happen to me and my wife, would you and your wife raise my children?" What an honor! They are saying, "Will you stand in my place? Out of love for me, will you extend the loyalty you have for me to my children and teach them the same values that we hold and that have drawn us together?"

One of these friendships formed twenty-two years ago and has remained strong to this day. My friend and I have wept in front of each other, shared hidden sin, confessed faults before each other, celebrated each other's victories, and been there for each other regardless of the circumstances. I have no reason to believe this will ever change until the day the Lord calls one of us home. In light of that inevitable day, we have asked each other, as an extension of our brotherly love and loyalty, to stand at the funeral and to celebrate the other's homecoming with the Lord.

Uncommon Disclosure

I have spoken with great regularity about the difficulties that are bound to come your way in life. I wish it were not so. I wish I could protect my sons from the waves that will crash on their lives. I cringe when I consider what they may have to endure. However, the longer I live, the more I know those moments are unavoidable. What makes them endurable is not walking through them alone. A band of brothers marked by full disclosure and true transparency will be the rudder that guides you through troubled waters.

In 1 Samuel 20:41, after they have discussed the real possibility that David's death may come at the hand of Jonathan's father, we read, "David got up from the south side of the stone and bowed down before Jonathan three times, with his face to the ground. Then they kissed each other and wept together— but David wept the most."

I admit I have not wept openly with many men, but I have with a few. I can't tell you how freeing and cleansing it is to let the emotions go. This is counter to how our culture believes a man should act. David W. Smith, author of *The Friendless American Male*, writes,

> Very early in life, little boys receive a cultural message that they're not supposed to show emotions. Expressing feelings is generally a taboo for males. Boys soon learn to

dread the words, "Don't be a sissy; big boys don't cry . . ." Other messages come through loud and clear—Boys have to learn to be men. And to be a man means you conceal your emotions.[14]

I have watched many young men bare their souls to their girlfriends or fiancées or men to their wives. This is not a bad thing at all. However, it is not healthy for a man only to disclose himself to a woman. Men need men. They need men just like women need women. Both sexes speak a language that is different from the other's.

When my wife tells me she needs girl time, I don't feel threatened by that statement. I don't feel threatened when she gets coffee with a close friend. I don't assume I'm blowing it because I can't meet her emotional, relational, or conversational needs. The truth is I can't fully meet all those needs. Part of it is because my own sin keeps me from seeing her needs more fully. The other part is that she speaks and needs to hear a language that is wonderful and beautiful and vitally important . . . but that does not come from my lips. When she returns from her time with the girls, I can tell how important it has been for her.

In many ways, women do this better than guys—way better. But it does not have to be that way. Being a man does not mean concealing your emotions. Being a man means fully disclosing who you are with honesty and transparency before your band of brothers. That kind of sharing will take your relationship to another level. As you give part of yourself away, you will find your band of brothers drawing closer. We don't tell each other what we feel because we are afraid of each other's reactions. Yet you will be amazed at how many struggles you share with your brothers to one degree or another.

I sincerely desire that you pursue deep and uncommon friendships as you progress through life. May these friendships be marked by the uncommon bond of shared values, by uncommon love, by uncommon loyalty, and by uncommon disclosure or transparency. If this becomes a reality, years from now you will look back with great satisfaction that you chose to invest in what you now call your *band of brothers!*

DISCUSSION QUESTIONS

1. If you have a band of brothers, how would you characterize your relationship and bond?

2. Would full disclosure characterize this bond? If yes, how so? If not, where are you holding back?

3. What was inspiring about the story of Staff Sergeant Salvatore Giunta? If your band of brothers were to resemble his company, what would you share and what actions would you take? Consider his words when he said, "They are just as much of me as I am."

4. If you do not have a band of brothers, whom might you seek out to develop a deeper friendship with that would be marked by an uncommon bond, love, loyalty, and disclosure? (Remember that shared values are the starting point of such a friendship.)

5. What hurdles does your band of brothers need to overcome to move your friendship(s) to the deeper level characterized by the four uncommon characteristics of friendship? Discuss.

6. What life struggles have you already experienced that have been endurable because of your band of brothers? Explain.

7. For those without a band of brothers, how might these events have been different if you had a close band of brothers? Tell your stories.

REACHING HIGHER

The questions above are good for self-reflection. However, if you want to get full value from them, answer them with the guys you consider your band of brothers or desire to have as your band of brothers.

Be honest with each other as you work through the questions. Ask each other if any of the four uncommon qualities of true friendship exist in your relationships. If not, why not? What should practically change (start or stop) for your relationship to become more like David and Jonathan's?

Talk it out . . . you will be glad you did!

"Does the road wind up-hill all the way?
Yes, to the very end.
Will the day's journey take the whole long day?
From morn to night, my friend."

—*Christina Rossetti*[1]

THE WRONG TRAIL

GUIDEPOSTS

* Without a godly trail guide, you may well lose your way.
* Sinful habits will deceive your heart and redirect your path.
* Be aware that the Enemy will strike at your specific weaknesses to destroy you.
* A renewed heart is marked by repentance and humility.

PRIOR TO MY SIXTEENTH BIRTHDAY, I purchased a Toyota 4x4 equipped with a double tubular roll bar, push bar, fog light, and large tires for "mudding." For a young man growing up in the mountains of Vermont, this was quite a ride!

Several weeks after my birthday, I was returning home from a driver's ed class one winter evening. Water had run off the side of the mountain onto the road and was freezing into black ice. Looking ahead, I saw the car in front of me fishtail but did not think much of it. As I rounded the bend, I felt my back tires suddenly begin to slide.

With seconds to spare, my choices were either to go off the side of the road to the right, which was a straight drop of thirty to forty feet, or else to steer very hard into a ditch on the other side of the road. Unable to correct the spinning, I turned the wheel in the hope of not going off the embankment on the right. Instead, I headed straight into the ditch. As the push bar on the front of my truck plowed into the embankment, my truck completely flipped and landed on its roof. It continued to slide upside-down for another twenty to thirty feet down the ditch.

Still buckled in my seat, I was shocked by how quickly I had lost control and ended up stuck upside-down in a ditch!

WANDERING FROM THE TRAIL

In the same way, how quickly life can spin out of control, especially when you don't have a trail guide walking with you on your journey. You can easily lose your way and end up so far off course that you hardly know how to find your way back to the trail.

Bernard Madoff, former American stockbroker, investment advisor, nonexecutive chairman of the NASDAQ stock market, and admitted operator of what has been described as the largest fraudulent investment scheme in American history, learned this lesson the hard way. After years of coverup, trickery, and deception, Madoff pleaded guilty to turning his wealth management business into a massive Ponzi scheme that defrauded thousands of investors of billions of dollars. A few months later, he was sentenced to 150 years in prison.

In his statement to the court, Madoff said that when he had started the scheme, he had expected to be able to end it quickly. Eventually he realized it would all catch up to him at some point, but he was in it so deep there was no turning back.[2]

In his article "The Downward Spiral of Sin," Jimmy Humphrey writes,

Sin is a terribly destructive thing. It always takes you further than you ever wanted to go. Often when we lie, we only intend on telling the lie once in order to alleviate us from whatever circumstance we feel is forcing us to hide the truth. You never intended on telling the second lie, but sooner than you know it, a second lie was told. And while you are probably not aware of it at the time, your sin is finding further inroads into your heart. And when this happens and it has a firm hold on your life, it keeps you longer than you ever intended to stay. How? The sin has become part of who you are as a person. It becomes part of your very character and nature. It now rules from the throne of your heart. You are now a liar.[3]

As long as you pursue something else instead of God, you will have all you want of sin until it simply consumes you. A great and terrible example of this is when Lot's wife ignored God's command to not look back as she and her family fled Sodom. She could not refrain from catching one last glimpse of those cities of sin. That simple glance backward literally cost the woman her life as she immediately turned into a pillar of salt.

Genesis 4:7 tells us of the gravity of sin: you must be on guard because "sin is crouching at your door; it desires to have you, but you must master it." This is why Paul urges you to "take captive every thought to make it obedient to Christ" (2 Cor. 10:5) and to "not conform any longer to the pattern of this world, but [to] be transformed by the renewing of your mind" (Rom. 12:2).

180 DEGREES

When we go down a wrong path, the Holy Spirit can convict us by revealing the sin in our lives. Sometimes the Spirit gently and powerfully moves in the quietness of our hearts.

Sometimes, however, only radical measures can snap us out of the condition in which we find ourselves.

The best example I can think of comes from the life of the apostle Paul. He was an aggressive and brutal Christian killer, a fanatical Pharisee, and an enemy of Christ. In Acts 9:1, we see Paul "was still breathing out murderous threats against the Lord's disciples." It wasn't until Paul was on his way to Damascus that the Lord began the transformation process by striking Paul blind. Although the Lord took away Paul's physical sight for three days, the Lord gave him spiritual sight so he could examine the nature of his own heart and see the grace and forgiveness God freely offered to him. As a result of his true repentance, Paul did a complete U-turn and went full speed ahead in the opposite direction. He moved from a life of killing Christians to a life lived for Jesus.

Years later, Paul described his struggles and his perspective following that change:

> Five times I received from the Jews the forty lashes minus one. Three times I was beaten with rods, once I was stoned, three times I was shipwrecked, I spent a night and a day in the open sea, I have been constantly on the move. I have been in danger from rivers, in danger from bandits, in danger from my own countrymen, in danger from Gentiles; in danger in the city, in danger in the country, in danger at sea; and in danger from false brothers. I have labored and toiled and have often gone without sleep; I have known hunger and thirst and have often gone without food; I have been cold and naked. . . . Who is weak, and I do not feel weak? . . .
>
> Therefore I will boast all the more gladly about my weaknesses, so that Christ's power may rest on me. (2 Cor. 11:24–27, 29; 12:9)

Even though you might stop in your sin, you are still close to that sin. Like Paul, you need to run in the opposite direction to pursue God and to do what he requires of you. Once Paul was converted, he had no urge to kill Christians again. That sin died with his old self! Paul sums up his commitment to Christ in Philippians 1:21, where he writes, "For to me, to live is Christ and to die is gain." Paul is saying it would be better to die and go to heaven; however, as long as God keeps him on earth, Paul will live his life for him.

Paul's case is a remarkable story of divine intervention, but it spills into a second applicable point. Paul recognized the importance of finding a younger man and speaking words of truth, wisdom, counsel, and accountability into his life. Shortly before his death, Paul wrote a letter to Timothy while he was in prison. He tells Timothy,

> You then, my son, be strong in the grace that is in Christ Jesus. And the things you have heard me say in the presence of many witnesses entrust to reliable men who will also be qualified to teach others. (2 Tim. 2:1–2)

Paul took deliberate steps so the gospel would be carried forward after he was gone. In turn, Timothy was faithful in listening and carrying out Paul's message of Jesus Christ.

We can quickly dismiss Madoff's story as out of our league—we could never be that bad! However, apart from the work of Christ and godly influences from others who cross our paths and redirect us, every single one of us has a Bernie Madoff heart. He never expected to get so far off the trail. His $20 billion fraud started with one unchecked sin that led to another and another until it was habitual. J. C. Ryle wrote,

> Habits like trees are strengthened by age. A boy may bend an oak when it is a sapling, a hundred men cannot root it

up when it is a full grown tree. So it is with habits: the older they are the stronger they grow. Habit is the nurse of sin. Every fresh act of sin lessens fear and remorse, hardens our hearts, blunts the edge of our conscience, and increases our evil inclination.[4]

THE FIRST THEFT

I personally experienced this in a way I will never forget. On my sixteenth birthday, I was walking through the grocery store and decided I would try stealing. As I made my way down the food aisle, I set my mind on a can of beef jerky. Looking over my shoulder, I saw only an elderly gentleman at the end of the aisle, so old I thought he probably couldn't even see me.

So, on December 2, 1986, I took a can of beef jerky and shoved it into my winter jacket. I briskly turned the corner and walked down the next aisle. Feeling very guilty, I glanced over my shoulder about halfway down the aisle and was shocked to see that the man had followed me and was gaining quickly. "Young man," he asked, "did you steal something and stick it in your jacket?"

Busted! Nervously, I admitted I had. He asked how old I was. I told him I was sixteen but did not mention I had only been sixteen for a few hours. I was too embarrassed to tell him this was how I had chosen to spend my sixteenth birthday.

I was not ready for what he said next! "Son, I am the owner of this store. Do you know I can press charges?"

"No, I did not realize that, sir."

When he asked who my parents were, I told him my father was the pastor of the church just down the road. "Tell you what," he said. "I'll give you ten minutes to run home and tell them before I call."

The important part of this story, however, is what occurred prior to this stealing incident. Over the previous months, my friend had introduced me to what he called the "five-finger discount." At first, I didn't know what he was going to do, but I will never forget the moment he did it. While I paid for my purchases at a convenience store, he shoved packs of gum and candy down his jacket. My heart beat so furiously I thought it would leap out of my shirt! Once we got out of the store, I verbally ripped into him for what he had done, telling him he should take back the stuff he had stolen.

This continued for some months. Before long, my heart no longer beat as quickly when he stole. Sin was becoming more comfortable. Even though I never did the actual stealing, I was right there with him. Just like Adam, who stood by Eve in the garden of Eden and silently did nothing as she ate the fruit, I too stood by and did nothing. What had happened to the convictions, the courage, and the strength I'd had when I'd aggressively confronted him that first night?

The more my friend stole, the more passive I became. His sin became my sin. Before long, I became the beneficiary of some of the goods he stole. He moved beyond gum and candy and began filling his jacket with cassette tapes, sometimes six or seven at a time. (Yes, I know tapes are old school!) Since we went to the same church and our parents were Christians, I thought we weren't that bad overall. I failed to take into account the negative effect he was having on me and slowly succumbed to his bad influence. Neither of us had the courage to take the necessary stand.

At the time, I considered the incident on my birthday to be my first theft. In reality, I had been involved in this sin for some time, although I had convinced myself I was innocent. The moment I had accompanied my "friend" on his second act of stealing marks the day I first stole. My birthday shoplifting attempt was simply the by-product of unchecked sin.

As I had followed my friend, I had begun to see the advantages of stealing without considering the dark side and potential results. Getting caught was the smallest of these consequences—the greatest issue was how my heart grew hardened as it became accustomed to sin.

The author of Hebrews writes, "And no creature is hidden from his sight, but all are naked and exposed to the eyes of him to whom we must give account" (Heb. 4:13 ESV). I forgot that God was fully aware of the sin in my heart and that Satan was having a field day with me!

J. C. Ryle describes how the Devil positions himself. He writes, "The devil will paint, and mask, and dress up sin, in order to make you fall in love with it. He will exalt the pleasure of wickedness, but he will keep out of sight the sting."[5]

That is exactly what happened to me.

A BRILLIANT DECEIVER

In his book, *When the Enemy Strikes,* Charles Stanley discusses our need to understand that Satan is not only real but is also seeking to steal, kill, and destroy! John 10:10 notes that from the beginning of time, Satan has been a master deceiver who was, and continues to be, very skilled at disguising himself. Paul tells us "we do not wrestle against flesh and blood, but against the rulers, against the authorities, against the cosmic powers over this present darkness, against the spiritual forces of evil in the heavenly places" (Eph. 6:12 ESV). Jesus said the Devil "was a murderer from the beginning, and does not stand in the truth, because there is no truth in him. When he lies, he speaks out of his own character, for he is a liar and the father of lies" (John 8:44 ESV). Paul further warns us when he says, "I am afraid that just as Eve was deceived by the serpent's cunning, your minds may somehow be led astray from your sincere and pure devotion to Christ" (2 Cor. 11:3). In *Triumph over Temptation,* John Owen writes, "Traitors occupy our own hearts, ready to side with every temptation and to surrender to them all."[6]

You need to know several important things about how the Devil operates.

He Strikes at Our Weaknesses

Please stop and consider: what are your areas of weakness? What do you most struggle with? What sin in your life can you just not seem to root out? The question is not *are* you going to be attacked spiritually, but rather *where* and *how!*

When Satan lost the battle against Michael and his angels, he and those in rebellion with him were thrown from heaven to earth. In fierce anger and furious rage, Satan has set about to make war with the woman and her offspring (Rev. 12:7–17).

In the book of Job, we see Satan looking to pick a fight. Instead of going after an easy target, he sets his sights on a man described as "blameless and upright, one who fear[s] God and turn[s] away from evil." (Job 1:1 ESV). Satan goes right after God's "best." When Satan arrives uninvited to God's council, God asks Satan where he came from. Satan responds, "From roaming throughout the earth, going back and forth on it" (Job 1:7 ESV).

No Christian is exempt from possible attacks by the Devil.

He Strikes When We Least Expect It

When your guard is down, Satan will come through the back door to attack you. That is why Peter says, "Be alert and of sober mind. Your enemy the devil prowls around like a roaring lion looking for someone to devour"(1 Peter 5:8). There is a war going on around you. The battle is over your heart! While the forces of darkness ultimately will be crushed because of Christ's work and resurrection, do not think you will be exempt from the harm they seek to inflict.

In the second film of the Lord of the Rings trilogy, Théoden, king of the horse warriors of Rohan, is fearful and reluctant to go to war. Meanwhile, an army is marching through his lands, intent on destroying all mankind. Villages fall; women and children are slain. Yet Théoden still balks, saying, "I will not risk open war."

Aragorn says, "Open war is upon you whether you would risk it or not."[7]

He Ensures That the Results Are Devastating

Satan does not care how happy you are as long as the end result of your sin is devastating. The Devil did not care how much stuff my friend and I stole or what momentary satisfaction it brought us as long as our minds were weakened, our hearts hardened, and our consciences seared. We were right where he wanted us.

When I look back at the time I stole, I see there was no man other than my father who really knew me and who was directly and consistently speaking truth into my life. I'm not trying to offload responsibility or shift the blame for my own wrongdoings, but I do believe that time in my life would have been different had another mentor been present to hold me accountable.

There are times when God provides for our needs, but we either fail to notice or else decline the assistance and accountability he offers. A Scripture passage I've used many times in my life comes from 1 Corinthians: "No temptation has overtaken you except what is common to mankind. And God is faithful; he will not let you be tempted beyond what you can bear. But when you are tempted, he will also provide a way out so that you can endure it" (1 Cor. 10:13).

Unfortunately, I allowed peer pressure and the "goods" of this world to control my eyes and heart instead of making Scripture the "light on my path" (cf. Ps. 119:105).

CRICKETS

While I was serving as the headmaster of a Christian school eight years ago, the school and I were on the receiving end of a young man's "strength gone bad." A senior decided that while everyone was attending an all-school chapel service, he would stop at the bait and tackle store. When we returned from the chapel, the custodian greeted me at the door to warn me about what I would find the moment I stepped inside. The young man had bought 5,000 crickets and set them loose in the hallways. To top it off, he had bought a dozen white mice and set them free in the building. The whole school was infested.

Turning around, I calmly went outside to where the students were waiting while the crickets were vacuumed up. I did not say a word. Instead, I simply began to look at eyes until I discovered the guilty party. Going to him, I told him to come with me, walked him into my office, and asked him why he had pulled the prank. He tried to play innocent and began to lie. I asked him again why he had done it. He again tried to act as if he did not know what I was talking about.

Finally, he broke. "How did you know it was me?"

It had been easy, I told him. His eyes had betrayed him. When I had walked out and surveyed the student body, he had barely lifted his eyes from the ground. When he had looked up, his eyes had been shifty, screaming, "I am guilty! I did it!" His look was similar to the look God must have seen on Adam and Eve's faces after the fall as they struggled with their nakedness and sin. In their shame, all they wanted to do was hide.

The prank itself was not the hardest part. In fact, now and then, I find it a bit humorous. The part that was most difficult for me was that I had invested heavily in this senior boy for a long time. I had coached him in fifth grade. During his junior and senior years, we had won two state soccer championships together. I had taught him in history class and had been his principal throughout middle school. In many ways, he had grown to be like a son to me. Over the years, I had needed to work with him during some ups and downs, but I had always been willing to engage in life with him.

This young man's final act before graduation was the legacy he chose to leave behind him. Someone had been speaking into his life for the past eight years, but he hadn't listened enough to stay on the right path. At the very moment when truth needed to triumph, he set aside our relationship and the time we had logged together in order to cover his tracks.

While I still care deeply about him and have many great memories of our time together, this was a frustrating moment for me. I very much wanted to see him "get it." Many times I have wanted to ask young men, "What will it take? What needs to happen to you in order for you to turn around and head back on the right path?" Then I have to catch myself before I get too focused on others and their own faults. I too have places in my heart where God is asking the same questions of me!

Repentance and renewal begins when each of us first examines his own heart. In the book of Proverbs, the author does not just offer words of wisdom but literally begs young men to listen to his words. Verses in Proverbs begin with, "My son . . . !" at least twenty times. Here are a few examples:

> Listen, my son, accept what I say,
> and the years of your life will be many. (4:10)

> My son, pay attention to my wisdom,
> listen well to my words of insight. (5:1)

> Now then, my sons, listen to me;
> pay attention to what I say. (7:24)

> Now then, my sons, listen to me;
> blessed are those who keep my ways. (8:32)

IT'S NOT TOO LATE

If you are running headlong down a wrong path, turn around. It is not too late! Reminding young men of this, J. C. Ryle wrote, "I grant you that true repentance is never too late. I grant you, one penitent thief was converted in his last hours, so that no man might despair; but I warn you, only one was converted, that no man might presume."[8]

You might think you, like Bernie Madoff, are in a situation so deep that you are not capable of finding your way to the right path. While we remain in our old self, this is correct. However, read the encouraging words of Paul. They are rich with hope, describing the new beginning Christ freely offers. Paul writes,

> And he died for all, that those who live should no longer live for themselves but for him who died for them and was raised again. . . . Therefore, if anyone is in Christ, he is a new creation; the old has gone, the new has come! (2 Cor. 5:15, 17)

> You were taught, with regard to your former way of life, to put off your old self, which is being corrupted by its deceitful desires; to be made new in the attitude of your minds; and to put on the new self, created to be like God in true righteousness and holiness.
>
> Therefore each of you must put off falsehood and speak truthfully to your neighbor, for we are all members of one body. (Eph 4:22–25)

C. S. Lewis puts it this way:

> Christ says "Give me All. I don't want so much of your time and so much of your money and so much of your work: I want You. I have not come to torment your natural self, but to kill it. No half measures are any good. I don't want to cut off a

branch here and a branch there, I want to have the whole tree down. I don't want to drill the tooth, or crown it, or stop it, but to have it out. Hand over the whole natural self, all the desires which you think innocent as well as the ones you think wicked—the whole outfit. I will give you a new self. In fact, I will give you Myself: My own will shall become yours."[9]

And in Ezekiel 36:26 God says,

I will give you a new heart and put a new spirit in you; I will remove from you your heart of stone and give you a heart of flesh.

As your journey continues, and you make your way on the right path, may you find the words of J. R. R. Tolkien a useful challenge and exhortation. After Faramir has nearly died in battle in *The Return of the King*, he lies unconscious until Aragorn brings him the cure that saves his life. Faramir wakens, slowly coming to his senses.

He spoke softly. "My lord, you called me. I come. What does the king command?"
"Walk no more in the shadows, but awake!" said Aragorn. . . .
"I will, lord," said Faramir. "For who would lie idle when the king has returned?"[10]

DISCUSSION QUESTIONS

1. Can you recall a time when you were heading down a path (a decision or course of action) that you should have avoided?

   a. What caused you to take the first step(s) down that path?

   b. Did you continue on that path? Why or why not?

   c. If yes, for how long?

   d. If you turned around, what caused you to do so?

   e. If you are still following that path, explain why you have not yet turned around. What would it take to make you do an apostle-Paul, 180-degree turnaround?

2. Have you ever tried to rationalize to yourself, as I did when my friend was stealing, that your path is not really so bad or could be worse? Explain.

3. If you have run in the opposite direction from the sin that you were pursuing, what have you run toward as a result?

4. How have you prepared for the Devil's surprise attacks that will be tailored to your weaknesses?

REACHING HIGHER

The first step toward the right path actually requires dropping to your knees in humble repentance! In Luke 15, Jesus speaks of heaven rejoicing when one sinner repents! In our language, a party we cannot begin to imagine takes place in heaven when we acknowledge our sin in humble repentance, seek forgiveness, and turn from our former ways.

The next step is to "confess your sins to each other and pray for each other so that you may be healed. The prayer of a righteous man is powerful and effective" (James 5:16). Open repentance and confession to the Lord, in the company of a brother or a band of brothers, will free your spirit, lighten your load, and prepare you to step forward onto the right path.

"This is what the LORD says:
'Stand at the crossroads and look;
ask for the ancient paths,
ask where the good way is, and walk in it,
and you will find rest for your souls.'"

—*Jeremiah 6:16*

STANDING AT THE TRAILHEAD

GUIDEPOSTS

* Many young men never venture on a journey toward their true biblical masculine design.
* You must take intentional steps to avoid becoming a "kidult" or a "boomerang" kid.
* In pursuing manhood, you must balance your contributions and your consumption.

I WISH I COULD SHARE the following thoughts with you in person as your trail guide. Face-to-face conversations trump every other form of communication man has created. It will take a humble heart and willing spirit to hear what I communicate in this chapter. That you have read this far is a good thing. If you can hear what I have to say in this chapter, it will prepare you for the rest of your journey.

As Aragorn said, you must no longer stick to the shadows, even though you may wonder where to go and how to get there as a young man. Past events in your life may have left you standing at the trailhead, uncertain if you even want to embark on this journey, wondering if you have what you need and if you will succeed should you choose to begin! If you have these concerns running through your mind, know you are not alone.

Without dismissing or excusing the uncertainty that may pervade this time in your life, I want to shed light on how we came to this place.

A NEW AGE

In Shakespeare's time, males were fully emancipated by the age of eighteen. As recently as 1970, the average age of successful emancipation was twenty. Today, the average age of successful emancipation is approaching twenty-seven.[1] This later period of emancipation may be connected to the developing concept of the teen years. In 1941, the word *teenager* was first used in a *Reader's Digest* issue.[2] Now, almost seventy years later, the parameters of the years before emancipation have stretched and the lines have blurred.

In January 2005, *Time* ran a cover article titled "Grow Up? Not So Fast." In the article, Lev Grossman describes how a new transitional stage has developed for many people in their late teens and twenties. During that time, they coast through life without gaining adult responsibilities, frequently changing jobs, often living with their parents for years after college. Such people have been called "kidults," "boomerang kids," and twenty-something Peter Pans![3]

CONSUMPTION AND CONTRIBUTION

For the moment, let me say much of this is the fault of our parents. (Before I become your hero, keep reading. You won't be able to use this as an excuse by the end of the chapter.) Often, well-meaning parents, attempting to provide for our every need, unintentionally hurt us in the emancipation

94

process. How? Because, up to this point, you might believe you can get something for nothing. John Rosemond, author of *Parenting by the Book*, strongly counters such logic by challenging every young man (and young woman) to consider the imbalance between his consumption and his contributions.[4]

For some of you, the imbalance might be radical. You might give nothing and get everything. This is not the real world. The very things you take for granted (like your bedroom, food, transportation to and from games, TV, video games, and other family resources) will be very costly once you strike out on your own. While these are great things that parents typically extend willingly to their sons, I ask you, "What have you done to offset costs or to contribute to your family's needs?"

My last two years of high school were spent at two different boarding schools. The school I attended my senior year was very strict concerning orderliness and cleanliness. After I had lived there about six weeks, the resident director approached me. He said he had been watching me closely and had noticed I kept a clean room and seemed to live a fairly disciplined life. He asked if I would be willing to have one of the underclassmen from the second floor move to my room. He thought I would make a good and helpful impression on him. He did a good job selling the deal, and I agreed.

When I went up to the young man's room to help him move, I was astonished by the sights I saw and the stench I smelled. I opened his closet doors to discover no clothes on the hangers, half-eaten snacks mashed amongst his clothes, and a hotpot covered with a thick blue layer of mold. When I opened his drawers, I did not find one item neatly folded. Instead, he had jammed dirty clothes into several drawers.

I took a deep breath, trying to decide between respectfully telling the resident director the deal was off or less respectfully telling the young man what a total slob he was. I chose neither option. Instead, I asked the student to leave the room, telling him I would handle the move myself and would let him know when I was done.

For the rest of that Saturday, I did all his laundry, folded his clothes, hung up his shirts and pants from dark to light, made his bed, and put the rest of his personal belongings neatly in drawers. When he walked into the room, he was shocked.

"There," I said. "I did it the first time; you will do it for the rest of the year, because I'm not getting any demerits because of you!"

The demerit thing was a huge external motivator for me. As long as students did not get twenty demerits or more and held a 3.0 or higher, they were exempt from the mandatory study hall period from 6:30–8:30 pm. This guy had gotten well over fifty demerits already. My greatest area of concern was the white-glove check conducted every morning. If clothes were found on the floor, beds were not made, furniture was not dusted, and so on, *both* roommates received demerits. His messes became my problem.

For three weeks, we did very well. However, my roommate soon realized I was not going to physically harm him in his sleep if he made us get demerits. Our perfect system began to crumble. He left dirty clothes on top of the dresser. I received "my" first demerits. Then it happened again! This had to stop. I did not want to lose the freedoms I had rightfully earned and enjoyed. I told my roommate that if he got any more demerits for us, I would take all of his clothes from the closet and drawers and dump them outside in the New Hampshire snow.

He probably didn't believe me, because only a few days later, he lapsed into his old pattern once again. With great vindictive pleasure, I made good on my promise. I will never forget the look on his face when he opened his closet to find nothing there. That look of astonishment was only outdone by his expression of shock when he looked out the window and saw his clothes in a heap on the ground.

I regret to say that the young man did not make it through the year. My best efforts, though manipulative and likely intimidating, had exposed a much bigger issue. One night, he told me he had never been shown, asked, or even told to do any of the things the school or I required of him. He had never needed to contribute to family life. He had grown up believing little would be expected of him. In his own words, I was the first person who had ever held him to a standard that would require him to be disciplined on a daily basis.

ARE YOU READY?

Today, many of our brothers have similar stories. Boomerang kids leave the house believing they are ready to strike out on their own, when, in reality, they have done nothing to prepare for the challenges they will face. Before long, they drop out of college, move back home, and try to get their feet back under them.

Before you quickly decide that could never happen to you, I ask that you consider a couple of questions. Your response will have specific ramifications for the next phase of your life.

Are You Responsible?

First, identify the areas of responsibility in your life. What contributions are you asked to make at home, school, and church without compensation? (Any job you hold is a wonderful thing, but since money is a great motivator, we need to leave it out of the picture for now.) What do you do to assist the common good in the arenas in which God has placed you? While much has likely been done for you over the years, you should see your contributions and your consumptions become more balanced as you near your emancipation.

97

Two years ago, my family had a difficult start to the summer. My three sons clashed over the smallest things and were not inclined to contribute around the house. Sensing we were heading in the wrong direction, I called a team meeting with the family and went over a contract I had written. The contract addressed my sons' chores, the schoolwork they would do over the summer to keep their minds sharp, the time they would get out of bed each morning, the ground rules for how much television they could watch, and the consequences for fighting with each other and borrowing from each other (which always led to a fight).

At the end of each week, my wife and I would sit down with the boys and evaluate the past seven days. If each son had completed his chores without complaining, had gotten out of bed at the required time, had completed his summer mind-sharpening exercises, and had not been sent to his room for violating the boundaries established for interpersonal conflicts, then he would get his allowance, receive three good meals each day, and be allowed to sleep indoors. Also, we promised to tell our sons we loved them each night before they went to bed.

About now, I suspect you are thanking Jesus you did not get me as a father! The meals and sleeping arrangements were meant to be tongue-in-cheek. The words "I love you" were unconditionally offered!

We established several things that summer. First, the older the son, the more work we required of him, and the more allowance we provided. Second, as our sons took more responsibility and contributed to the family, they began to realize just how important their contributions were to the greater good of the family.

The culmination of this understanding came when we re-roofed our house. From my wife to my three sons, we made it a family project. Our bonding came not so much through the roofing and the hundred bundles of shingles I dragged up the ladder, but through our conversations, camaraderie, encouragement, conflict resolution (a roof is not a great place to have conflict between sons), and the satisfaction we felt when our task was done.

Working together can make for great memories. In fact, my second son Josiah, seven at the time, gave up the opportunity to play with his friends so he could roof with his dad. In a contemplative moment, he stood up and exclaimed, "This is so much fun, Dad! I hope I can do this for the rest of my life!"

Are You Willing to Die to Yourself?

Consider looking at your family with a new perspective. Your family is a team, even if it does not look like any team you have known or joined. I am always telling my sons they are on Team Brower. They should take pride in that team and should do everything in their power to make their team successful. As a young man, your first step is to understand your role and consider how you might lay down your life for your other family members.

You might think I have gone overboard. You thought this book was about you and your journey, but now it sounds like a book on parenting. In reality, I am making this point specifically for you. I am calling you to fully surrender your deep desire to be served and instead to do what Jesus did for his thirty-three years on earth at the will of his Father.

The apostle John writes, "By this we know love, that he laid down his life for us, and we ought to lay down our lives for the brothers" (1 John 3:16 ESV). Needless to say, this has been a very unsettling verse in my home. My boys understand 1 John 3:16 on a head level. The problem is they see laying down their lives as a one-time event instead of a daily denial of self for others.

99

While some are called to physically die for Christ, most of us are called to deny our fleshly desires. As you begin to do this, others reap great benefits from your selfless acts, and you become the beneficiary of rich blessings! This is much like short-term mission trips. Rarely do the people who go on those trips give more than they receive. Without a doubt, they give much to others and their gifts are deeply appreciated. However, by engaging and serving, they start to see the world as Jesus saw it.

Approaching family life in this manner prepares you for greater challenges to come. In addition, you reduce your chance of becoming a "boomerang kid" after you launch your emancipation departure. You don't want to leave home only to find yourself unable to achieve the life you always wanted. To prevent that, practice a life of responsibility, stewardship, and servanthood, starting today!

LIVING AND GIVING—NOT TAKING

Some years back, I knew a young college student who lived with a group of peers in a house off-campus. They had agreed to throw in money to purchase groceries and to share the cooking and cleaning responsibilities. For almost his entire senior year, this guy was a "freeloader." He never held up his end of the bargain, while the rest of his housemates did their share and more.

Unfortunately, "there is no such thing as a free lunch." Someone must pick up the tab! At first, the other guys in the house carried the burden. However, the one who paid most dearly was the freeloader. After graduation, he got married, had a couple kids, and has struggled to hold down a job ever since. While his buddies thought they were helping him out by flipping the bill week after week and by doing jobs he should have done, they were actually enabling him. He began to think this lifestyle would actually work for him. The best thing that could have happened to him during his senior year would have been for those other guys to have held him accountable and, at some point, given him an ultimatum.

Imagine yourself in this situation. What words might you have offered him? At the time, this young man needed his band of brothers to hold him accountable, to impress on him the value of good hard work, and to recognize the Lord requires nothing less of us.

In Colossians 3:23–24, Paul describes the mindset we should have as we go about our work.

> Whatever you do, work at it with all your heart, as working for the Lord, not for men, since you know that you will receive an inheritance from the Lord as a reward. It is the Lord Christ you are serving.

This perspective alone should radically change how you view work and how you must address the motivations behind what you do.

Douglas Bond, author of *HOLD FAST in a Broken World*, said it well when he wrote,

> A young man who works for his divine Employer will do his work with excellence. There's no room for shirking when you work for the King of kings. And you will be most productive and profitable when you work to please your divine Task-master. When praised for a job well done, you will shift the praise back to your Master. You will tell others that you were able to accomplish such a great task only with God's tools, on his time clock, and with his training and encouragement.[5]

One Saturday afternoon, I wanted to rush out the door but had to wait for my wife who was intent on finishing the meticulous task of cleaning our home. In my state of impatience, I foolishly said, "It's not like the president is coming over—come on, let's get going."

"Hey, that's not fair," she said. "You're always talking about how everything we do must be done for the glory of God. I am cleaning for the glory of God!"

That's it! She was right on! What was I thinking? A task is not great based on its appearance but rather based on the motivation of our hearts. Needless to say, I was convicted and compelled to shut my mouth, jump in, and start helping.

Being fully invested and committed makes all the difference. When your heart, head, hands, and feet are working in unison, you will find the journey a worthy adventure that must be pursued.

DISCUSSION QUESTIONS

1. Evaluate the degree of balance in your life between your consumption and your contributions. Are there adjustments you can make to better prepare yourself for what lies ahead?

2. Based on the three areas of needed preparation prior to leaving your home (degree of responsibility, service to your family members, and pursuing excellence in all you do for the glory of God), evaluate whether you are a candidate to be a "boomerang kid." (This may take some time of reflection and serious evaluation. However, it will be time well spent.)

   a. Share what God is revealing to you about yourself.
   b. What adjustments must you make?

3. Do you have a close friend who is a self-serving freeloader well on his way to becoming a boomerang kid? If yes, how

can you take steps to help him steer away from that result? (Be sure to take care of your own business as well. You can be right on point but wrong on presentation. Be gracious in your approach.)

REACHING HIGHER

Even if you find there is a fair balance in your personal consumption and contribution, go ahead and tip the scales! Increase your contributions! Help the family member who would least expect it . . . and then go and help again! Be sure Mom is included!

Don't wait to be asked. Take the initiative and when credit is given, humbly deflect it outward and upward.

Make this a habit—Scripture tells us it is better to give than to receive!

"The trail is the thing, not the end of the trail. Travel too fast and you miss all you are traveling for."

—*Louis L'Amour*[1]

BACKCOUNTRY ADVENTURES

GUIDEPOSTS

✳ The desire for high adventure lies within you.

✳ In your journey toward manhood, you must either accept or decline the invitation to true adventure.

✳ You must be vigilant not to fall for counterfeit adventures that will distract you from your true journey.

WATCHING MY THREE sons play reminds me of what life was like when I was growing up. For them, a limit is made to be stretched, a boundary to be stepped across, and a record to be broken. For example, one evening, some friends were visiting when their young son came in and said that Josiah, my nine-year-old, was on the roof. Going outside, I saw it was not enough for Josiah to eat his dinner *in* the tree fort I had built my sons—he had to be *on top* of the tree fort, sitting on the roof with his plate on his lap. I still can't figure out how he got his food to the top of the tree fort some twenty-five feet off the ground.

Skateboard and bike ramps are prevalent on our property. We have a zip-line from the tree fort designed for a single rider.

However, my sons have attempted to see if three people can hold on the entire way without falling off. Cuts, scrapes, and bruises are honor wounds, a worthy price to pay for the feats attempted and mastered.

While we were dating during my college days, my wife got some foreshadowing of what life would be like should we ever have a house filled with sons. One warm fall afternoon, we went with a group of friends to a rock quarry where we enjoyed cliff-jumping some 30–40 feet into the water. On this particular visit to this quarry, we noticed someone had set up a long zip-line over the water. I volunteered to go last—not out of fright but out of pride. I hoped to let everyone ride the line and drop in the water before I tried some crazy move to impress everyone, especially my girlfriend.

My wife-to-be, who had already jumped from a local bridge some fifty feet above the water, found this an easy feat. She grabbed the handle of the zip-line, took off running, and, releasing her grip on the handle, gracefully entered the water. I thought, "How cool is it that my girlfriend likes this kind of thing!"

When my turn arrived, I figured I had to up the ante. I set my mind on doing a back flip that would end with a beautiful dive to the applause of my friends and the admiration of my girlfriend. As I headed over the quarry, I failed to take into account the speed at which I was moving and the trajectory at which I would be entering the water. As I went into my back flip, I realized this was not going to go well. I over-rotated and came down on my face and stomach from about thirty feet in the air. There were parts of my body that did not react kindly to that type of impact.

Visibly, I was a mess. I had fractured a small bone under my eye. The fracture allowed air to pass into the sinus cavity, causing immediate swelling to the point where I couldn't see out of my right eye. The doctor told me not to worry; the problem would soon fix itself. For the next week, I walked around campus looking like I had been in a horrible fight. Not only did I look foolish, but my pride took a beating because I did not even have a great story to explain why my eye was swollen shut.

FINDING THE GOOD ADVENTURE

You may have stories of adventure where risk, danger, and a rapid heartbeat are necessary ingredients. Your strength may have been put to the test, and you may have come away feeling like you had conquered the world during the hike, the climb, or the adversity you overcame.

Your adventure might not have been a blood-rushing, pulse-pounding, heart-stopping experience. Instead, it might have involved a peaceful walk as creation shouted out the glory of God: water rushed over rocks, birds sang their songs, thunder rolled in the distance, lightning struck powerfully, or majestic mountain ranges stretched before you, impossible to replicate with a paintbrush. Seeing, hearing, and almost tasting such beauty refreshes the soul and revives the spirit.

As you consider your own story and the times when you underwent great risk, faced significant danger, pressed on through an ordeal, evaluated which adventures to repeat or to never try again, or took a quiet walk to reflect on God and your life, you will find these experiences indelibly burned into your memory. The pursuit of adventure is just part of how we have been designed by God.

DETOURS AND DIVERSIONS

At this point, some of you might be ready to put down this book because you can't relate. Possibly the greatest adventure you have had has been behind the joystick of the latest video game. That's because, for all practical purposes, video games have replaced baseball as a young man's favorite pastime. According to a 2007 study, the average eight- to twelve-year-old male spends sixteen hours a week playing video games. And this amount *rises* as they grow older—teenage males spend an average of eighteen hours a week gaming.[2]

While my focus in this chapter is not mass media, television, and movies, I do believe video games are a major issue worth reviewing. Consider the amount of time and money being spent on video games. You need look no further than *Halo: Reach*. When this game was released on September 14, 2010, revenue reached $200 million on its launch date alone.[3] In 2008, video game sales topped $21 billion![4] Great time and resources have been invested in video gaming.

At this point, you might be on the defensive. You may conclude you are not addicted to video games, gaming is just a hobby, and there are much worse things you could spend your time doing. And, of course, you are certainly not as bad as that guy who plays way more than you do. Please, hear me when I say I am not condemning video games wholesale. However, if you are self-disciplined to the point where you spend very little time engaged in video gaming and can shut off a game as easily as turn it on, consider yourself in a small minority.

Let's examine some lifestyle-altering questions that may help you to sift through the decisions you make regarding gaming. Beyond the money, consider the amount of time you spend playing games. In a five-day week, most young men have approximately twenty-five hours of "extra" time to spend. (I arrived at this number by subtracting eight hours a day for sleep, eight hours a day for school, and three hours a day for meals. That is likely generous.) How do you account for the five extra hours a day?

If you are spending a large amount of time playing video games, you must ask yourself, "How is this preparing me in my pursuit of godly masculinity?" If this is your greatest adventure, what have you achieved when you get the high score? Have you strengthened your body in any way? Have you deepened any relationship in a lasting way? What real obstacles or area of adversity have you tackled head-on? Have you learned valuable life lessons through triumph or defeat? In the hours you spend gaming, what are you *not* doing?

Every time we say yes to something, we say no to other things. If you are spending twenty-three hours a week playing video games, you must ask yourself what you are giving up. When you turn the game off and real life resumes, are you able to affirm your strength and your masculinity? When called on, will you have the confidence to offer your strength when needed? If you are a heavy user of video games, you are likely ill equipped for such a task.

I do not believe God made us to sit behind a video game for twenty-three hours a week—or even two to three hours a day. Young men, you are being called to a much greater adventure, one that will require more from you than pushing buttons with your thumbs.

A NOTE OF CAUTION

Clearly, I am encouraging certain life pursuits while extending great caution toward others. To present a balanced perspective, we should ask ourselves whether some real-life adventures could become extreme to the point where they too are addictive and unhealthy! Adventures can have a shadow side as well.

People vary on a good definition for *extreme sports*. At minimum, my definition would include the fact that a strong adrenaline rush is associated with them; if not, the activities can become dangerous and lead to injury or death (hence the word *extreme*).

A friend of mine told me how, in his younger days, he pursued kayaking to the point where it almost killed him. As he mastered each maneuver, he felt he had to push the limits time after time. While in his early twenties, he found himself on the Upper Gauley River in West Virginia just after the winter snow had melted. At no other time of year do the rapids of this river have the depth, volume, and intensity of rushing water.

The Upper Gauley River is wild and unpredictable, and only expert rafters or kayakers should attempt these Class-V rapids (Class-V being the highest level of difficulty). However, David was full of adventure and thought highly of his trained abilities. On this particular trip, he found himself broached (or broadside) to the current. As he hit the next major hydraulic (a place where the water backflows at the base of a ledge or rock), the kayak capsized. Turbulent water thrashed his body while the kayak was upside-down. After what seemed like eternity, he was able to finally roll his kayak upright. Despite losing his paddle, he made his way to the side of the river. At the time, he was thinking, "Why am I doing this?"

This is a good question. Each of us must ask it on a regular basis. Is an adventure all about that next thrill or rush of adrenaline, or does a transcendent cause beckon you?

TRANSFERABLE COURAGE

Remember the quote at the start of this chapter: "the trail is the thing, not the end of the trail." The actual adventure matters less than the life lessons learned along the way.

I have learned a lifetime of lessons from watching my seven-year-old son, Jakob. Today, I was amazed as I watched him crawl under the barbwire fence to offer some breakfast to two of our neighbor's horses. He stood dwarfed yet courageous beside those monstrous animals as he held out his hand, offering them his morning pancakes.

You might think this was stupid because he could have gotten trampled. (In this case, I agree, and I called him to come back.) However, several weeks ago at the senior retreat that gave me the impetus to write this book, I saw a courage in him that many seniors wished they possessed. On the last night, the students had an opportunity to stand and speak to their classmates around the bonfire. Jakob, who had accompanied me on the trip, nudged me and said, "Are there really 106 seniors here?"

"Yes, there are, son."

"Wow."

After a brief thinking pause, Jakob said, "OK, Dad—I want to say something." After he cleared his speech through me, he stood in front of those big seniors, which was not much different from standing between the two horses, and courageously said, "I want to say thank you for letting me come on this trip and to say thank you for so many of you being nice to me."

That took guts! I admired my seven-year-old son for his boldness and his courage!

I don't know what God has in store for Jakob. According to him, he is going to be a missionary to China. When his older brother asked him, "You know they kill missionaries in China?", he didn't blink an eye or hesitate as he quickly replied, "That's OK! Someone has to tell them about Jesus!" Much of this is how God has wired him. Some of it has been through my wife's and my efforts as his parents to say yes to his adventurous life when no seemed like the safer way to go.

I do recognize there are limits to always saying yes. But always playing it safe will leave you in a secluded room with a video game machine, chasing after a fantasy life that will leave you less alive than before you started. One day, you will wake up and ask yourself, "Where did my life go? What have I done that counted for anything worthwhile?"

GOD DOESN'T ASK YOU TO PLAY IT SAFE

How does all this apply to practical life scenarios? Look what happened when some noteworthy men in the Bible attempted to play it safe. Adam went passive just when his wife and the entire human race needed him the most. Warrior-king David should have been with his troops in battle; instead, he was walking on his rooftop watching another man's wife take a bath. Even after God showed Moses several miracles to prove he would be with him, Moses was afraid to speak to Pharaoh and lead the Israelites. Abraham, fearful for his own life, referred to his attractive wife as his sister when powerful men looked at her with interest. When God called Jonah to Nineveh, he fled in the opposite direction!

However, Elijah engaged in a face-to-face stand-off against the prophets of Baal. While still a young shepherd, David ran at 9'9" Goliath armed with nothing but a slingshot. Joseph could have slept with Potiphar's wife, but instead he fled and ended up in prison. Moses could have lived in luxury as a prince of Egypt, but "he chose to be mistreated along with the people of God rather than to enjoy the pleasures of sin for a short time" (Heb. 11:25). He refused to stand by and watch his people, God's chosen people, be beaten and abused. Daniel had the courage to obey God and refuse to pray to a human king, even though he knew the lion's den awaited him. Jesus did not play it safe when he gave up his throne, came to earth, took all our sins on himself, died, and went to hell and back for us!

As you continue on your journey, you must hear and work to apply several core statements to your life. These will equip you better for the journey ahead.

Know Who You Are

I just described many men who had courage and an adventurous spirit. They knew who they were and were sure of their connection to the Great King. What about you? Do you know who you are? The answer to this question changes everything. Princes and paupers have a different view of themselves, their value, their worth, and their place in this world. God does not just call us his servants or his friends—he calls us his sons! How empowering to be a son and an heir of the Great King!

Paul writes,

> And because you are sons, God has sent the Spirit of his Son into our hearts, crying, "Abba! Father!" So you are no longer a slave, but a son, and if a son, then an heir through God. (Gal. 4:6–7 ESV)

To be a slave is to be in bondage, to be oppressed, but to be a son of the King—can you imagine the privilege, the opportunity, the freedom?

Observe God's Handiwork

Draw close to God so you can hear him talking. How is he speaking to you? What direction does he want you to take? Are you listening? In Psalm 16:11 (ESV), the psalmist writes,

> You will make known to me the path of life;
> in your presence is fullness of joy;
> at your right hand are pleasures forevermore.

Reflect, Reflect, and Reflect!

Learn more about yourself as you reflect on God's goodness, his character, and his plan for your life. In Ephesians 2:10, Paul writes, "For we are God's workmanship, created in Christ Jesus to do good works, which God prepared in advance for us to do."

This is a profound statement. "God's workmanship" implies we are his masterpiece, his best work, but it gets even better. He allows us to enter into a greater story than our own: his story.

Paul says God has given us good works to perform, works ordained before the foundation of this world. When we complete these works, we must give God the credit so we cannot boast in our own efforts! If God has ordained that these works be done, he will make a way for us to accomplish them! How empowering! If God is for us, who can be against us? (Cf. Rom. 8:31.)

Fully Rely on God

When your strength fails, you are in a great place! We see men in Scripture who found their strength failing them but who knew where to go for renewal and revival.

> Do you not know?
>   Have you not heard?
> The Lord is the everlasting God,
>   the Creator of the ends of the earth.
> He will not grow tired or weary,
>   and his understanding no one can fathom.
> He gives strength to the weary
>   and increases the power of the weak.
> Even youths grow tired and weary,
>   and young men stumble and fall;
> but those who hope in the Lord
>   will renew their strength.
> They will soar on wings like eagles;
>   they will run and not grow weary,
>   they will walk and not be faint. (Is. 40:28–31)

John Calvin wrote, "Seeing that a pilot steers the ship in which we sail, who will never allow us to perish even in the midst of shipwrecks, there is no reason why our minds should be overwhelmed with fear and overcome with weariness."[5]

Be Disciplined

You will need to be disciplined as you apply and work at what God has been teaching you. The apostle Paul framed this matter well when he wrote,

> Everyone who competes in the games goes into strict training. They do it to get a crown that will not last; but we do it to get a crown that will last forever. Therefore I do not run like a man running aimlessly; I do not fight like a man beating the air. No, I beat [discipline] my body and make it my slave so that after I have preached to others, I myself will not be disqualified for the prize. (1 Cor. 9:25–27)

Notice the purpose in these words. We too carelessly refer to our Christian life as a walk. I would contend it is more than that—not a walk or a sprint but a marathon. John MacArthur further elaborates on this point when he says,

> Most people, including many Christians, are instead slaves to their bodies. Their bodies tell their minds what to do. Their bodies decide when to eat, what to eat, how much to eat, when to sleep and get up, and so on. An athlete cannot allow that. He follows the training rules, not his body. He runs when he would rather be resting, he eats a balanced meal when he would rather have a chocolate sundae, he goes to bed when he would rather stay up, and he gets up early to train when he would rather stay in bed. An athlete leads his body; he does not follow it. It is his slave, not the other way around.[6]

In 1 Timothy 4:7–8, Paul says,

> Train yourself to be godly. For physical training is of some value, but godliness has value for all things, holding promise for both the present life and the life to come.

115

This is where following Jesus becomes hard. John describes how some of Jesus' disciples left him because they hungered for the sensational. They wanted to see miracles performed. When Jesus said he was the only spiritual food they needed, their reactions revealed the condition of their hearts:

> From this time many of his disciples turned back and no longer followed him.
> "You do not want to leave too, do you?" Jesus asked the Twelve.
> Simon Peter answered him, "Lord, to whom shall we go? You have the words of eternal life. We believe and know that you are the Holy One of God." (John 6:66–69)

Are you willing to embark on the greatest adventure yet, where God asks you to deny yourself and to take up your cross and follow him (Matt.16:24)? In *Absolute Surrender*, Andrew Murray wrote, "We find the Christian life so difficult because we seek for God's blessing while we live in our own will."[7] C. S. Lewis said in *Mere Christianity*, "The more we get what we now call 'ourselves' out of the way and let Him take us over, the more truly ourselves we become."[8]

When we deny ourselves, we find ourselves. With such a perspective, you are now ready to engage in serious trail conversations!

DISCUSSION QUESTIONS

1. Evaluate how you spend your free time. Do you spend it challenging, strengthening, or stimulating your mind, body, and spirit—or are you cast into a catatonic, mesmerized state as you stare at a TV or a computer screen?

2. As you evaluate how you are currently spending your time, identify those things you are neglecting or choosing not to pursue that actually may be of great benefit and service to you and others.

3. How did godly men like Adam, Moses, and Abraham respond in situations where they chose to follow their own selfish desires instead of following God? How did each of these counterfeit adventures backfire on them? Can you think of other examples from the Bible?

4. The five core statements at the end of chapter 7 are intended to better prepare you for your journey ahead. Which of these five core statements do you best understand and implement in your life? Which of these statements do you struggle with the most? Where is the most difficult struggle? What will it take to address the area(s) of struggle?

REACHING HIGHER

Unplug! You decide what you will choose, but choose something . . . maybe get radical and unplug it all! Yes, I know what I'm asking of you. I have plenty of gadgets available at a moment's notice. However, I challenge you to walk away from your gadgets for a day! Do it, and then wrestle with question #4.

This may be a good challenge for you and your band of brothers. Be sure to get together and compare notes. What did you think about? What did you hear? What conversations did you have with God or with even yourself? Yes, get unplugged. You might like it.

(If, at the end of the time, you feel like you are going stir-crazy, know you may be addicted to your electronic devices and need more time away from them. At least, that's what I discovered!)

PART 3

ESSENTIAL TRAIL CONVERSATIONS

"I went to the woods because I wished to live deliberately, to front only the essential facts of life, and see if I could not learn what it had to teach, and not, when I came to die, discover that I had not lived. I did not wish to live what was not life, living is so dear; nor did I wish to practice resignation, unless it was quite necessary. I wanted to live deep and suck out all the marrow of life, to live so sturdily and Spartan-like as to put to rout all that was not life."

—Henry David Thoreau[1]

We have left the trailhead long behind and are well into our journey. Imagine now that I am your trail guide who is walking with you, having conversations about real-life issues. Our journey together must come to an end at some point, so I will be deliberate about what I share with you.

The selective heart-level issues I have chosen to discuss are absolutely essential for every young man. You will struggle with these issues if you do not receive and heed direction and instruction. I know this from my own experience. In addition,

I have observed and engaged with many, many young men like you who have battled with these very matters.

So, if I might say in the words of Solomon, "Now then, my sons, listen to me; pay attention to what I say" (Prov. 7:24). Or, in the words of our Great King during his discourse with Job in Job 40:7, "Brace yourself like a man"!

> " 'For this son of mine was dead and is alive again; he was lost and is found.' So they began to celebrate."
>
> —*Luke 15:24*

POSITION VERSUS PERFORMANCE

GUIDEPOSTS

- ✳ Too often, a man finds his value and self-worth in the approval of others.
- ✳ Your perceived competence will lead to a life of either avoidance or pressure to perform.
- ✳ As a son of the Great King, you cannot earn or lose his favor!

I RECENTLY ASKED eight senior guys in the small group I lead, "What do you fear?" Immediately, guys started to talk about their fear of failure and fear of not measuring up. One young man, who has played on the varsity soccer team for the past three years, said, "When I was Most Valuable Player of the district and First-Team All-State as a sophomore, I thought my junior year was going to be easy. However, I found myself feeling so much pressure to perform and measure up to everyone else's standard."

All eight of the guys are varsity athletes. When I asked how many of them had ever wanted to walk away from their sport, each one raised his hand. I asked them, "Then why don't you?"

To a man, every one of them said that, between the expectations of others and personally finding their worth and value in their sport, they just could not do it. What bondage! To play begrudgingly or out of a sense of obligation is no way to play a sport or to live your life.

Our chief end should be to glorify God and enjoy him forever. However, somewhere along the way, we have written our own creed that says we must please others and ourselves . . . at all costs! If that is our motivation, we should consider stepping back or away from what we are doing for a period of time until we can refocus and engage for the right reasons.

BIGGER, FASTER, STRONGER

Today, life for many young men sounds like this: bigger, faster, stronger, quicker, make that grade, make that squad, get into that college, get the high score, score the most points, get that job, hit that home run . . . the list can go on and on. Somewhere along the way, we have bought into the belief that these things make up our identity and reputation and complete our résumé, our record, and who we are. Ultimately, we allow those things to define our lives.

As a result, we take two basic approaches to life. First, because of our fears and apprehensions, we try to reduce or eliminate people, situations, and events that cause us fear and anxiety. Some of you might have had this experience in the past. You went out for a team and got cut, took a class and failed, tried to hang with a certain group and got rejected. Your answer to these common problems is a life of avoidance. For you, avoidance seems safe. You don't want to risk anymore. Instead, you make very calculated moves. By avoiding the potentially negative responses you so fear, you believe you can control the outcome. Sure, you might not be the most exciting guy, but this kind of life is predictable, and, for you, it's safe.

Alternately, you may have found moderate or great success in the things you have attempted to do. You have received applause, pats on the back, "attaboys," and feedback such as "nice work," "keep it up," and "way to go, champ!" The only problem is that when tomorrow comes, you will have to rise and do it all over again. People's expectations and standards are exceedingly high. Heaven forbid you ever dip below that bar.

Like the guy who avoids risks, you too seek to control your outcome; however, this is a different situation. You've got skill! Yet, the pressure, often self-inflicted, is great—sometimes overwhelming. You are supposed to excel, you are supposed to do well, and if you do—good, just keep it up! If you fail, you get more attention for your failures than you generally did for your successes. For example, if you have been blessed to get all As and only one B on a report card, what happens when your parents see the grades? Often, they focus on the one B, trying to figure out where you went wrong and why you didn't get an A in that particular class as well.

Over and over, I have had young men tell me how they experience the never-ending pressure to be bigger, faster, stronger, and smarter. When they are not able to meet the mark, they feel discouraged, feel like a failure, and feel trapped, not knowing where to turn. In the movie *Chariots of Fire*, a great example of this comes when, in a reflective moment, Harold Abraham says, "I am twenty-four, and I've never known [contentment]. I'm forever in pursuit, and I don't even know what I am chasing . . . . And now, in one hour's time, I will be out there again. I will raise my eyes and look down that corridor, four feet wide, with ten lonely seconds to justify my whole existence. But will I?"[1] Can you hear the anguish and deep sadness in these words?

Later, the same character tells his fiancée, "If I can't win, I won't run." She wisely responds, "If you don't run, you can't win!"[2]

THE RIGHT WAY OUT

Whether you are living a life of avoidance or taking a moralistic, keep-it-up, "try harder" approach, you find yourself enslaved to the constant, entangling fear that either you don't measure up or you do . . . at least until tomorrow. Unfortunately, I believe this is part of our hardwiring as human beings. It was the trouble that Adam and Eve fell into—reaching, wanting more, wanting to control their environment and situation.

In Romans 8:15–16, Paul offers us words of great hope. He writes,

> For you did not receive a spirit that makes you a slave again to fear, but you received the Spirit of sonship. And by him we cry, "*Abba,* Father." The Spirit himself testifies with our spirit that we are God's children.

You must not miss what Paul is saying here. We don't need to find our identity in performance, records, reputation, résumé, achievements, or outcomes; our identity does not depend on what we have done but rather on our position in Christ. We are adopted! In fact, Paul uses this word several times throughout his letters to drive home that point.

You might wonder why this is so important. Why didn't Paul just say we are sons of God, as is said in other parts of the Bible? Paul uses the powerful analogy of adoption because, in Roman culture, adoption provided special security. A father could disown his biological child, but a legally adopted child would remain an heir for life. No one could change this legally binding agreement![3]

What does this mean for you as a young man? If you are struggling with a life of avoidance because you feel you don't measure up, or if you have a just-work-harder mentality, you must not fear any longer. Stop running! Stop trying to prove your worth based on your own merit or good works. You are a son of the great King Jesus! You have been chosen, permanently adopted, and irrevocably changed. You were born a slave with great reason to fear, but now you have been adopted into the family of God and have great reason to hope and trust. This is the rich and lavish story of the gospel.

How well you think you can perform on a particular task probably affects your approach to it. If you think you can't perform well enough, you will avoid it at all costs. However, if you think you can perform well, you will work hard to do a great job that you want credit for. You believe you should be applauded and awarded for a job well done. Now that we are adopted sons, our Father's competence is what is important—not ours. Our security rests in what our Dad (God) can do! We boast in Christ and not in any great thing we did.

Our worth before God does not change based on our performance. Instead of performing, our focus changes to faithfulness. We don't need to win favor—we already have that! We are called to be faithful with what God has entrusted to us.

PRESSURE TO PERFORM

Seven years ago, I was driving back from a soccer game with Joshua, then six years old. That particular Saturday afternoon, Joshua had scored four goals. Such results were not abnormal for him, because God has blessed him with athletic abilities. However, he had not been as offensively productive in a game the week before, and I must have somehow indicated I was not as pleased with his "performance."

After his four-goal blitz, Josh in all sincerity turned to me and said, "Dad, do you love me more now since I scored four goals this week?"

You might as well have driven a knife through my heart. I immediately thought, "Did I say or do something last week that made him make such a statement?" Then I wondered, "Does he bear the weight of that pressure to perform for his dad and for his dad's approval?"

I immediately pulled the car over to the side of the road, for such statements are serious attention-getters and demand a sincere response. I put my hands on his shoulders, looked him dead in the eye, and said, "I love you and will always love you, even if you never score another goal or pick up another soccer ball."

I don't know if he could have fully expressed it at the time, but I believe that was very freeing for him to hear. Having coached high school varsity soccer for the past eighteen years, I have seen young men absolutely hate the game for the simple reason that their fathers were always telling them all the ways they could improve.

This past weekend, I watched a young man on Josiah's club soccer team have to endure two sets of parents (the result of divorce) yell orders and commands that at times even contradicted each other. I started to make a mental list of their demands: pass the ball, dribble the ball, just shoot it, listen to your coach, pick your head up, get back on defense, don't be a quitter, don't sulk, and on and on . . . I saw the young man look at his coach and look at those two sets of parents, and my heart bled for him. He was working his heart out. By the end of the game, he was emotionally spent just from trying to make everyone happy. This young man could crash and burn someday because there is no way he can measure up. He is killing himself trying to make everyone happy.

I wanted my son Josh to know the pressure is off. With my words of reassurance, I told him, "There is nothing you can do to gain or lose my love, to earn or lose my favor. I love you unconditionally regardless of your successes or failures." My hope was that he felt free to enjoy life to the fullest while using God's gifts to bring glory to God. Even if he had an off day or did not meet his personal standards or the expectations of others, he could walk away without feeling like a failure, because he had worked and played to faithfully steward what God had entrusted to him.

What would you attempt to do if you knew you could not fail? This is what the gospel is about. God says, "I love you regardless!" He said that even though our best efforts are as filthy rags to him. Quit trying to earn favor. Jesus paid the price.

In Jesus' parable, the prodigal son comes home to be a servant, trying to prove his worth to his father through his offer of service. His father meets him and in essence says, "No, you are not going to work for me—it is not necessary. This is not about your performance; it is about your position! Have you forgotten your position? You are *my son!*"

DISCUSSION QUESTION

1. Where have you felt the pressure to perform? What influencing forces have applied this pressure?

129

2. Where are you successful in life? What are those areas where you receive the most praise and affirmation?

3. How would you respond if recognition for a job well done in your area of giftedness suddenly stopped? Explain.

4. Are there areas in your life where you feel approval is inseparably tied to what you do? What are these areas?

5. What would you attempt to do if you knew you could not fail?

6. What effect might it have on your life and what you pursue if you fully believed, in the depths of your being, that you are unconditionally loved despite your performance? How might this transform the way you pursue your areas of giftedness?

REACHING HIGHER

Review your answers to question 1. As you look at the list, know you likely need to change your mindset. For example, athletics (and virtually every other area of life) can be boiled down into four elements of training: technical, tactical, physical, and emotional/mental. Unfortunately, the mental side of athletics is rarely trained even though people often talk about it. I believe the mental aspect affects everything; get this wrong and not much else goes right. I often remind my players that mental is to physical as four is to one. In other words, you might be physically as fit as a stallion, but if your mental state and preparation is weak, you will probably be ineffective.

Before you begin any activity on your list, change your mindset from "success according to statistics" to faithful stewardship of what God has entrusted to you. Leave outcomes to him. You focus on the process or, in our case, the journey! The Great King wants to see your faithfulness with your giftedness and receive the glory for a good outcome. (You might now have the courage to tackle your answer to question 5 with your new mindset.)

"The books or the music in which we thought the beauty was located will betray us if we trust to them; it was not in them, it only came through them, and what came through them was longing. These things—the beauty, the memory of our own past—are good images of what we really desire; but if they are mistaken for the thing itself they turn into dumb idols, breaking the hearts of their worshippers."

—*C. S. Lewis*[1]

"Those who cling to worthless idols forfeit the grace that could be theirs."

—Jonah 2:8

WHAT'S IN YOUR BACKYARD?

GUIDEPOSTS

✳ Your heart is made to worship . . . something.

✳ Whatever captures the affection and attention of your heart serves as your functional master.

✳ The Lord or lords of your life will define your life journey.

ONE OF MY FAVORITE STORIES is the call of Gideon in Judges 6. First, the angel of the Lord comes to him, and says, "The LORD is with you. O mighty man of valor" (v. 13 ESV). I am not sure how that statement hits you; however, since I just finished talking about performance and self-worth, I believe hearing those affirming words from an angel would be quite motivating. Yet, just like Moses, Gideon immediately begins talking about his weaknesses and his inadequacies. Despite God's promise to Gideon—"I will be with you, and you will strike down all the Midianites together" (Judg. 6:16)—Gideon still doubts, so God patiently gives him multiple signs to prove he will keep his promise to help him.

Sandwiched between the call of Gideon, the fleece test, and Gideon's 300 men defeating the entire Midianite army, the Lord gives Gideon a command to obey before he goes into battle: tear down his father's idols. Under the cover of darkness that night, Gideon pulls down the idols and replaces them with an altar to the true God. This takes great courage. When morning comes, men of the town want to kill Gideon for his action.

IDOLS OF OUR OWN

We may hear this story and quickly assume people were messed up back in those days. Seriously, no one worships gods like this anymore. I would beg to differ. Before you skip over this chapter, hear the words of D. M. Lloyd-Jones: "An idol is anything in our lives that occupies the place that should be occupied by God alone. . . . An idol is anything by which I live and on which I depend, anything that . . . holds such a controlling position in my life that . . . it moves and rouses and attracts so much of my time and attention, my energy and money."[2]

Before I sound like I have it all together, I humbly admit I have struggled immensely with idolatry over the years. This problem doesn't just go away when you get older; it takes some serious intervention. Some of my idols have been my sons and their accomplishments, my possessions, approval from others, identity-driven performance or success in coaching and work, having others be dependent on me, being in control, earning another degree, and the list goes on.

In *Counterfeit Gods*, a book I highly encourage you to read, Tim Keller writes, "An idol is whatever you look at and say, in your heart of hearts, 'If I have that, then I'll feel my life has meaning, then I'll know I have value, then I'll feel significant and secure.' "[3] These types of relationships can best be defined in one word: worship!

We cannot break any of the last eight commandments without violating the first two: "You shall have no other gods before me" (Ex. 20:3) and "You shall not make for yourself an idol in the form of anything in heaven above or on the earth beneath or in the waters below" (Ex. 20:4). These commandments are clear in their comprehensiveness, yet, in my sin, I try to justify the things I pursue and assign great value and worth by giving them my time, attention, and affection.

CHOOSE POORLY, PAY DEARLY!

Dealing with the idols of the heart is an ongoing process, not a one-time event. The human heart is never neutral—it must worship something. It constantly elevates other people and things above God and worships them. As a result, we must always look for the reasons behind our attitudes, actions, and sin. What is the sin behind the sin? God doesn't reveal the idols in our lives just to be mean. Instead, he approaches us gently—like a father—so we can live in freedom rather than slavery (Gal. 4:9). Too often, we ourselves address only the symptoms but neglect the root cause.

Every idol has unbelief at its core. We don't like to talk about it, but that is the reality. We do not believe God alone is sufficient; we do not believe we can find meaning and lasting fulfillment in him. How do we change this? We must commit ourselves to grace. Christ died to "get you." Everything else will demand that you purchase it. You must have a greater love for God than for your idols. Falter now, and you will turn around in twenty or thirty years and ask yourself if you have gained anything of lasting and eternal value.

We have spent significant time talking about the *wrong* path in your journey. The longer you go down that path, the more difficulty you have turning around. Think of when we get lost. Instead of asking for directions, we keep driving and driving and driving. (Guys, for some reason, we are horribly guilty here.) All the while, we are moving farther and farther away from our true destination.

It is time to stop and figure out who will be the true Lord of your life. Otherwise, you will run a race you can never win, because you will never cross the nonexistent finish line. The so-called American Dream and our "right to the pursuit of happiness" have been the downfall of many men who went before you.

This is an urgent matter. Joshua emphasized its importance to the Israelites when he said, "Choose for yourselves this day whom you will serve" (Josh. 24:15). Why was this such an important message? Joshua knew the Israelites were surrounded by heathen nations whose ways would look awfully attractive to them. Scripture gives us the rest of the story. Joshua was right on. In a very short time, the Israelites did "as they saw fit" (Judg. 21:25). They chose poorly and paid dearly. J. C. Ryle wrote, "Young man, do not be deceived. Do not think you can willfully serve yourself and your pleasures in the beginning of your life, and then go and serve God with ease at the end."[4]

Ask yourself this question, "Am I currently on the path I desire to follow into my adulthood?"

SEARCH AND DESTROY

The following questions are designed to help you to discover the idols in your life that rob you of God's joy and cause temporary spiritual insanity.

- What keeps you going?
- What preoccupies you?
- What is your greatest nightmare?
- What do you worry about most?
- What makes you feel the most self-worth?

- What are you proudest of?
- What do you really want and expect out of life?
- What do you think would make you happy?
- What, if you failed or lost it, would cause you to feel you did not even want to live?
- What do you rely on or comfort yourself with when things go wrong or get difficult?
- What do you think most easily about?
- What does your mind turn to when you are free?
- What prayer, if unanswered, would make you seriously consider turning away from God?

As you work through these questions, look for common themes. What functional masters guide or dictate your life? What things are too important to you? As you identify your idols, stop and ask yourself what happens when someone messes with them. For example, one of my idols is control. My house is my castle. I believe I deserve a peaceful home where my sons don't fight, where they listen to and respect their mother, and where they do what I ask the first time I ask it. When the "subjects" in "my kingdom" defy my expectations, I cannot believe it. In a self-justified and self-righteous anger, I act in a way that communicates to people, including my family members, that they are either vehicles to accomplish my goals in my kingdom—or else obstacles to those goals. What restrictive tyranny, and what a far cry from the words I piously recite on Sunday mornings when I say the Lord's Prayer: "Your kingdom come, your will be done on earth as it is in heaven" (Matt. 6:10).

Ask yourself, "What happens when someone messes with my idols or my little empire?" After Gideon destroyed the idols in his backyard, "the men of the town demanded of [Gideon's father], 'Bring out your son. He must die, because he has broken down Baal's altar and cut down the Asherah pole beside it' " (Judg. 6:30). Wow! How dear were their idols to them, and how dear are our idols to us? Is your response, "Someone has to die today!"? You will know how dear your idols are to you when you begin tracking your emotions. After you find yourself blowing up, clamming up, overreacting, etc., ask yourself what brought you to that point.

Every idol-system is a way of works-salvation (back to the whole issue of performance) keeping us "under the law." When we refuse to rest in Christ's salvation, we are driven to find our own. Stop looking to the counterfeit. Realize that you are righteous in Christ, and the idol's power over you is broken. Paul writes, "For sin shall not be your master, because you are not under law, but under grace" (Rom. 6:14).

Repent of your idols, give up your self-declared authority as the ruler of your little empire, and live free in the saving work and love of Christ!

DISCUSSION QUESTIONS

1. What are the things in your life about which you think, as Tim Keller wrote, "If I have that, then I'll feel my life has meaning, then I'll know I have value, then I'll feel significant and secure"?[5]

2. If you are wondering whether something is an idol, walk away from it for a period of time. How might you respond if it was removed from your life for a day, a week, or a month? What things hold you captive by their power?

3. To press further, what areas are off-limits to others? What are those things in your life that people have to pay for messing with . . . someone has to die?

4. Write down how you spend your free time. Do you notice areas in your life where you spend *extreme* time?

5. As you search your heart, ask yourself what idols or little empires you need to surrender to God and ask for release from their power. (Talk about this with others, as you will need accountability and prayer for victory over the things that have power over you.)

REACHING HIGHER

This chapter goes directly for the jugular. If you have answered the questions above, you likely feel rather exposed. I know the feeling. If there ever was a time, now is the time to call for backup. You need accountability from brothers, trail guides, mentors, youth pastors, and anyone else who can help you identify what you worship. The lure of our functional masters can be so strong and so controlling that it makes it hard for us to see or think straight, let alone evaluate our own hearts.

Allow those closest to you to see your answers to the questions above. Let them talk out what you should walk away from and walk toward instead.

Finally, in humble reliance on God for strength, with Christian accountability, begin this new leg of your journey.

> "Many inquire who is the greatest in the kingdom of God, who know not whether they shall ever be numbered among the least."
>
> —*Thomas à Kempis*[1]

JUST BEFORE THE FALL

GUIDEPOSTS

* ✳ Pride is a competitive relationship destroyer.
* ✳ In humility, you must count others more significant than yourself.
* ✳ The gospel of Christ frees you to humbly admit weakness and brokenness.

IN THE FALL OF 2001, expectations soared for the high school varsity soccer team I was coaching. In 1998, we had been the state runner-up, and in 1999 and 2000, we had won two state championships back-to-back. Before the year began, players and parents alike were talking about a "three-peat." Concerned, I wondered how much success and attention our players could take before it had a detrimental effect on their attitudes and ultimately their play.

Only several games into our season, I was notified that we were ranked #23 in the nation by the USA Today Adidas soccer poll. Of course, the players were thrilled. Later that weekend, we played in a tournament at Jekyll Island, Georgia, where top teams from Georgia, Florida, and North Carolina were also playing. We went up against two teams that were above us in the national rankings and successfully shut out both of them. In short, it did not take us long to shoot up to a #3 national ranking.

That year, we had twenty shutouts and only surrendered two goals right up to our last match. However, with each shutout and every new ranking, it became more and more difficult to motivate the team to work hard and not become complacent. Most thought we were a shoo-in for the state championship that year. The season came to an abrupt end, however, when we lost 1–3 in the regional championship match.

Looking back, I wonder if it would have made a difference for us to go through the season without the press, rankings, attention, and hype that surrounded the team that year. As much as I tried to talk about being thankful for our God-given abilities, humble about our successes, and appreciative for the recognition, it was a lot of attention for a group of sixteen- to eighteen-year-old men to handle.

PROBLEMS WITH PRIDE

While athletic successes and accomplishments can certainly puff up one's pride, problems with pride extend beyond athletics. C. S. Lewis framed this notion well when he said, "[Pride] is competitive by its very nature. Pride gets no pleasure out of having something, only out of having more of it than the next man. We say that people are proud of being rich, or clever, or better looking than others. It is the comparison that makes you proud: the pleasure of being above the rest."[2]

Remember our discussion on idols. Often, the things that others have make us the most discontent. We think we would be content if only we had . . . something else. However, when we get what we so desperately desire, we are not satisfied with simply having the same as the next guy. Now we want *more* so we can say we are the best and have the most. C. S. Lewis says that pride "comes direct from hell. Pride is spiritual cancer; it eats up the very possibility of love, or contentment, or even common sense. The essential vice, the utmost evil, is pride."[3] James quotes Proverbs 3:34 when he writes, "God opposes the proud but gives grace to the humble" (James 4:6). I am constantly talking to my athletes about this issue. I ask them to search their hearts for any pride the Lord needs to deal with personally. Otherwise, we as a team may suffer the consequences alongside the individual.

We see this happen in the Old Testament when the Lord dealt with the entire camp of Israel because of the sin of one man. In Joshua 7 and 8, Joshua sends soldiers against the nation of Ai. What looks like an easy victory for the Israelites turns into a rout as the Israelites flee back to their camp, defeated and humiliated. Joshua soon learns the reason for the defeat: despite God's order that all plunder from Jericho be destroyed, a man by the name of Achen had stolen some goods. Because of his disobedience and idolatry, Achen and his family are stoned to death. His sin had not just affected him and his family but the entire nation of Israel.

At the conclusion of our 2011 soccer season, we lost the state championship in a shootout. I find myself asking, "Is it I, Lord? Is there unrepentant sin in my life that you are dealing with on a much grander scale?" We out-shot the team 15-3 and were the favorite to win, yet God didn't see fit to give us the victory.

Many might think this is over-spiritualizing an athletic contest. I'm not so sure. I believe we do have to at least lead with that hard question. *Is it I? Is it something in my heart?*

In like fashion, I am appalled at how much egocentric trash talking goes on with athletes. In 2006, after a rival from across town defeated us 3–2 on our field, their star player told the newspaper, "I love to come and play here and win on this field." Since that time, we have defeated them almost every year in the district championship. Every year, players have said, "Coach, just say in the paper how much we like to win on their field." I don't need to respond; they know we are not even going there.

DOWNFALL OF A KING

We see a prime example of arrogance in Daniel 4. In that account, the Babylonian king, Nebuchadnezzar, proudly walks about his palace, admiring his kingdom. "Is not this great Babylon, which I have built by my mighty power as a royal residence and for the glory of my majesty?" he asks himself (Dan. 4: 30 ESV).

What is the consequence of such arrogance and pride? Daniel 4:31–33 (ESV) says,

> While the words were still in the king's mouth, there fell a voice from heaven, "O King Nebuchadnezzar, to you it is spoken: The kingdom has departed from you, and you shall be driven from among men, and your dwelling shall be with the beasts of the field. And you shall be made to eat grass like an ox, and seven periods of time shall pass over you, until you know that the Most High rules the kingdom of men and gives it to whom he will." Immediately the word was fulfilled against Nebuchadnezzar. He was driven from among men and ate grass like an ox, and his body was wet with the dew of heaven till his hair grew as long as eagles' feathers and his nails were like birds' claws.

Nebuchadnezzar was restored after seven years. A changed man, he said these words: "Now I, Nebuchadnezzar, praise and extol and honor the King of heaven, for all his works are right and his ways are just; and those who walk in pride he is able to humble" (Dan. 4:37 ESV).

Are we any different? We achieve some degree of success, and we quickly revert to the posture of King Nebuchadnezzar. "Look at what I have done!" I have watched athletes post comments on Facebook about their personal accomplishments the very night their football team was beaten by fifty-plus points. What's up with that? Terrell Owens, the professional football player, makes a touchdown catch, takes a pen from his sock, and signs the very football he just caught. Seriously? Doesn't he get paid millions of dollars to catch footballs? J. C. Ryle said, "Pride never reigned anywhere so powerfully as in the heart of a young man. Pride makes us rest satisfied with ourselves, thinking we are good enough as we are."[4]

Over the years, I have watched many freshmen come into training camp. I can tell a lot about them based on how much they talk. One year, we had a young man come into camp; the only thing he could talk about was how well he had done in the last training session. The players got fed up with him, and news soon reached me of what he had been saying. I had to pull him aside to let him know how turned-off the team was by his attitude. It needed to change. Boastful words are not what we are about.

GIVING YOURSELF AWAY

The humble person looks at what he can do better. He is always learning and striving, knowing he will never fully arrive. However, the proud and arrogant person is always passing the buck, pointing the finger, and blaming someone else if something goes wrong. He is deceived in his heart and mind, thinking he is above fault, above error, and above correction.

The infamous news conference with NBA basketball star Allen Iverson is a prime example. His coach was disciplining him for missing practice. In response, he publicly belittled his coach's decision during a live interview. "I'm supposed to be the franchise player, and we're talking about practice. . . . not a game. . . . How silly is that?" When someone asked him how he might make his teammates better by being at practice, he replied, "How in the hell can I make my teammates better by practicing?"[5]

Iverson conveyed his belief that he was above practice. His teammates might have needed the extra work but not him—he was good enough. From what I have observed, as well as from speaking with many coaches, the most talented player on the team is rarely the hardest worker on the team. Pride closes our ears against all advice and does not permit us to see shortcomings that are very clear to others.

Contrast Iverson's prideful and self-centered approach with the following illustration. Since 2001, I have taken three trips with my soccer team to an orphanage in Acapulco, Mexico. It might sound like a vacation in disguise—unless you see these guys in action. I watched them work tirelessly as they carried buckets of rocks, mixed concrete by hand, poured concrete walls, and helped build a new dormitory. In fact, I watched the guys make concrete by mixing mortar, sand, and gravel together by hand. All the while, an electric cement mixer sat just a few feet away from them. The Mexican foreman, Pedro, insisted we not use the cement mixer but mix the cement with shovels.

The boys learned a valuable lesson about missions that day. Instead of complaining, they realized their role was to sacrificially give their lives away instead of trying to "fix" the way the locals went about construction work. After hours of hard labor, they played with about sixty orphans. They showed the love of Jesus in remarkable ways.

From these trips, we learned that mission work is countercultural; it humbly puts others' interests before our own.

That trip drove us to live so that we could not see other people without viewing them through Jesus' work on the cross. Missions gave us insight into a world we knew existed but had never dared to enter. It allowed us to engage the ugliness and brokenness of the world by acting in a redemptive manner. We learned it really is more blessed to give than to receive. We experienced the joy of giving our lives away for others—we loved it!

WHO'S SIGNIFICANT?

It is so helpful for high school students to engage in mission-oriented work. Don't think you need to go to a foreign country; working with a local community service organization is just as beneficial. Getting our eyes off ourselves and rubbing shoulders with those who are not like us can give us a healthy dose of humility.

Nor should your mission field be limited to community service organizations. It is no secret the day-to-day rhythm of school life can cause an extreme focus on the self. Too often, life in high school revolves around self-preservation and self-promotion . . . regardless of the expense to others around us.

Humility means considering others more significant than yourself. However, high school students assign value to other people based on good looks, intelligence, athleticism, charisma, popularity, and so on. For those not counted "worthy" by the masses, this is a brutal time that can have immobilizing, emasculating effects on young men. I have seen many want to quit their journey, succumbing to the belief that this must be what life is all about.

You don't need to figure out who people are and how they rank. Instead, ask yourself what you count them to be, and then consider how the Lord views them. Is your view consistent with God's?

John Piper asks, "Will you count other people worthy of your service! Worthy of dying for, worthy of going down and lifting them up, worthy of taking interest in their affairs, will you count them that whether they are that or not!"[6] Stop the pretending, stop the hiding, and simply ask Jesus to give you a new heart and a new spirit. Ask him to take away your stony, stubborn heart and give you a responsive heart (see Ezek. 36:26). The more we see our flaws, our shortcomings, and our sin, the more powerful and electrifying the truth of the gospel becomes to us.

What might God be asking you to do? Are you willing to experience his work in your life? Are you resistant? What change needs to happen in your heart? Can you begin by simply admitting that you are weak, that you are broken, and that you desperately need a Savior each and every day?

DISCUSSION QUESTIONS

1. What is the difference between being thankful for what you have done, accomplished, or been given versus being filled with pride over the very same things?

2. Where in your life do you find yourself acting like King Nebuchadnezzar?

3. Where do you, maybe unknowingly, assign value and worth to the lives of others? Who? Be specific. Why do you do this to them? What is your basis?

4. Have you ever been moved to give of yourself for another whom you have considered unworthy of your time, attention, and affection? Explain the situation and the response from the receiver, as well as your feelings as the giver.

5. As you consider the value you place on people, what might God be calling you to do that may cause you to feel internal turbulence? Be honest with yourself.

6. Lest this become a good-works box-checking exercise, ask God to expose and deal with those areas of pride in your heart that elevate self above others. Discuss these areas with your band of brothers.

REACHING HIGHER

Review your answers to question 3. If you want to truly enliven your journey, go and be with those you have assigned minimal value or worth. After all, didn't Jesus come for the sick, the wounded, and the brokenhearted? How might you also be about his business?

Before you go, make sure your perspective is correct. Remember, you are not helping these people because they desperately need you, but because you desperately need them. You must do what Jesus did: "he humbled himself and became obedient to death" (Phil. 2:8).

This, young men, is what dying to self is all about!

"Forgiveness means bearing the cost instead of making the wrongdoer do it, so you can reach out in love to seek your enemy's renewal and change."

—*Tim Keller*[1]

11

NO PAYBACKS?

GUIDEPOSTS

 ✳ Forgiveness (given and received) will be a necessary part of every relationship you enter.
 ✳ When you are hurt, getting even or withholding forgiveness will not bring you healing.
 ✳ Showing forgiveness and grace may actually cause you to suffer as the offended one.

IF YOU CAN INTERNALIZE the words you read about burning away your pride and admitting you need Jesus, then you are ready to hear my next point. However, if you are defensive, making excuses, pointing the finger, and just trying to even the score, my words will be difficult for you. Only the person with a "broken and contrite heart" (Ps. 51:17) will be able to read about true forgiveness and then apply it in his dealings with others.

Willingness to forgive is an absolute prerequisite for any relationship you enter. You will need to both extend and receive forgiveness because you will both offend and be offended. Even the best of friends will have to maneuver through this difficult and often rocky terrain.

From birth, we want to pout, sulk, and ultimately get even with those who wrong us. A toddler whose toy has been taken or a spouse whose marriage has been rocked by unfaithfulness will have the same unsanctified response. "Somebody's got to pay. Until we are even, I will give blow for blow, loss for loss, pain for pain; I will not relent."

This is a very dangerous place to find yourself. Hurt people turn around and hurt other people, and the evil multiplies. The initial victim becomes the offender and the offender becomes the victim. We must reject equivalency and realize an eye for an eye will never compensate for the loss suffered by the first. In *Forgive and Forget: Healing the Hurts We Don't Deserve*, Lewis Smedes writes,

> The problem with revenge is that it never gets what it wants; it never evens the score. Fairness never comes. The chain reaction set off by every act of vengeance always takes its unhindered course. It ties both the injured and the injurer to an escalator of pain. . . . Why do family feuds go on and on? . . . The reason is simple: no two people, no two families, ever weigh pain on the same scale.[2]

SPOT THE DIFFERENCE

Growing up in northern Vermont, I saw a vivid but sad example of this as an early teenager. Our closest neighbors owned a thousand-acre farm divided between two families. They feuded over everything possible: from the proceeds of the milk and maple syrup they produced to what pieces of land belonged to them. Eventually, their feuding got so bad that they had to milk the cows on a rotation.

When one of the wives became ill, her dying wish was for peace between the brothers. She told her husband the feuding was not worth it, nor was it becoming of two Christian men.

Heeding his wife's counsel, the man took a small portion of the land and surrendered his rights to the rest. But instead of admitting he was in the wrong, the other brother took more than his fair share of everything.

The feud made an indelible impression on me in three ways. First, I found the animosity between these two brothers confusing and even frustrating. Though I never had a brother, I always thought I would not have acted in such a way. Second, I saw how possessions and pride are great tools of the Devil, used to drive wedges between families. Third—and most striking—was the fact that these were two Christian families that professed the name of Jesus. Oh, the wasted years!

Often, Christians and non-Christians seem to handle conflict very similarly. Former slave-ship captain and converted English clergyman John Newton explained how you, as a Christian, should think of the people who offend you:

> If he is a believer, in a little while you will meet in heaven; he will then become dearer to you than the nearest friend you now have upon earth. Anticipate that period in your thoughts. . . . [If he is an unconverted person,] he is a more proper object of your compassion than your anger. Alas! He knows not what he does. But you know who has made you to differ.[3]

A PAINFUL RESTORATION

In *The Reason for God*, Tim Keller writes,

> Forgiveness means refusing to make them pay for what they did. However, to refrain from lashing out at someone when you want to do so with all your being is agony. It is a form of suffering. You not only suffer the original loss of happiness, reputation, and opportunity, but now you forgo the

consolation of inflicting the same on them. You are absorbing the debt, taking the cost of it completely on yourself instead of taking it out of the other person. It hurts terribly. Many people would say it feels like a kind of death. Yes, but it is a death that leads to resurrection instead of the lifelong living death of bitterness and cynicism.[4]

As a school leader, I have learned that being emotionally hurt is part of the job description. I have received anonymous letters, had plenty said behind my back, and even people close to me have said and done things that cut me deeply. However, some would say I have done the same to them.

In one case, a third party let me know that one of my faculty members felt minimized and unvalued, so we agreed to seek counseling. When the first session began and issues were laid on the table, I realized I had hurt the person by my actions or lack thereof. I confessed I had not cared for the person as well as I should have, apologized for the pain I had caused, and asked for forgiveness.

I left the session feeling weary but encouraged by what had taken place. However, as time wore on, no follow-up meeting ever happened. While the relationship has improved, I had to ask the Lord to take my heart to a place where a response from the other party was not necessary. I had said what I needed to say, and I knew if I didn't leave it there, bitterness and resentment would set in. I still felt hurt for a period of time, however, because I did not feel a complete restoration in the relationship had taken place.

Forgiveness always costs us something. Instead of getting revenge or making demands, we are called to suffer. This type of grace and forgiveness is unfashionable, almost unheard of, and undesirable to most. It is hard to swallow. However, I found the following sentences from Lewis Smedes most helpful. In *The Art of Forgiving: When You Need to Forgive and Don't Know How*, he writes,

Spoken forgiveness, no matter how heartfelt, works best when we do not demand the response we want. I mean that when we tell people we forgive them, we must leave them free to respond to our good news however they are inclined. If the response is not what we hoped for, we can go home and enjoy our own healing in private.[5]

NEVER A SURE VICTORY

Most of us like the temporary satisfaction of getting even, making someone pay. But does that really improve our situation? Do you not still have that empty pit in your stomach, telling you something is just not right? Of course you do. You have not done what God wants from you.

AT&T recently came out with a commercial in which a teenage girl calls a teenage guy. The conversation goes something like this:

Jen: "Hello, Todd. I am just calling to let you know that I am giving you the silent treatment."

Todd: "So you are calling me to tell me you are giving me the silent treatment."

Jen: "Um . . . yeah."

Todd: (sigh) "Jen, this is like the eighth time you have called. . . . I don't think you understand how the silent treatment works."

Jen: (silence)

Todd: "Jen . . . Jen . . ."[6]

The first time I saw this commercial, I thought it was a funny commercial. The second time I saw it, I said to myself, "That was me, you idiot! That is what I used to do." While I was dating my wife, and even very early in our marriage, if I was upset about something or took offense, I sometimes gave

155

her the silent treatment. It was my passive-aggressive way of getting even. I thought it would be a sure victory for me. Yet I remember lying in bed, telling myself, "Just say something," and hoping she would break the silence. In my stupid pride and stubbornness, I thought I was winning . . . but knew all along that my chosen path would lead to loss and failure if I didn't turn around quickly. Although I wish I could rewind time, my gracious wife has been quick to forgive me of such childish behavior.

Don't get caught up in such foolishness in your own relationships. As God reconciled us to himself through his Son, so we too should be reconciled with each other. Reconciliation begins to heal a ruptured relationship. While the relationship can never go back to its original state as if the problem had never happened, forgiveness should allow it to move to an even more healthy condition. Smedes writes, "Forgiving what we cannot forget creates a new way to remember. We change the memory of our past into a hope for our future."[7]

POWERFUL FORGIVENESS

From 1948–1994, the South African government adopted a brutal system of racial segregation called *apartheid*, which ripped the country in two. After apartheid ended, grace, forgiveness and healing needed to take place. But where does a nation begin? Apartheid had caused so much pain and bloodshed; much physical and emotional damage had been done over the decades. Nelson Mandela, elected to the presidency after twenty-seven years in prison, believed he needed to forgive in order to heal his country. He could have called for vengeance and retribution against the whites. Instead, he called for forgiveness. He turned to Desmond Tutu, then Archbishop of Cape Town, and asked him to chair the Truth and Reconciliation Commission, where victims of violence could tell their stories and where perpetrators of crimes could ask for amnesty.

The 2009 movie *Invitcus* illustrates Mandela's philosophy when he says, "Forgiveness liberates the soul. It removes fear; that is why it is such a powerful weapon."[8] When his chief guard asks why white men are still allowed on the president's select police service, Mandela says, "The Rainbow Nation starts here. Reconciliation starts here. Forgiveness starts here."[9]

The Truth and Reconciliation Commission allowed opportunities for some truly amazing stories of forgiveness. A particularly noteworthy one is below.

> Many of the atrocities were truly horrific. A policeman, by the name van de Broek, told of how he and his fellow officers shot an 18-year-old youth, then burnt the body. Eight years later they went back, took the father, and forced his wife to watch as he was incinerated. She was in court to hear this confession and was asked by the judge what she wanted. She said she wanted van de Broek to go to the place where they burned her husband's body and gather up the dust so she could give him a decent burial; van de Broek agreed. She then added a further request, "Mr. van de Broek took all my family away from me, and I still have a lot of love to give. Twice a month, I would like for him to come to the ghetto and spend a day with me so I can be a mother to him. And I would like Mr. van de Broek to know that he is forgiven by God, and that I forgive him too. I would like to embrace him so he can know my forgiveness is real." Spontaneously, some in the courtroom began singing Amazing Grace as the elderly woman made her way to the witness stand, but van de Broek did not hear the hymn; he had fainted, overwhelmed.[10]

Suddenly, the idea of paybacks sounds rather trivial, does it not? Remember the words of Jesus:

For if you forgive men when they sin against you, your heavenly Father will also forgive you. But if you do not forgive men their sins, your Father will not forgive your sins. (Matt. 6:14–15)

Smedes wrote, "To forgive is to set a prisoner free and discover that the prisoner was you."[11] You'll know forgiveness is taking hold of you when you call to mind those who have hurt you in the past and find yourself wishing them well!

That is the freedom Smedes is speaking of, and it is the freedom Christ offers us.

DISCUSSION QUESTIONS

1. If you are like me, you may want to begin naming those people who have hurt you and should be asking you for forgiveness. This is the wrong starting point. I challenge you to first ask, "Where have I already been forgiven?" Or, better yet, is there a time when someone could have demanded you pay but instead chose to forgive you? How did that make you feel? This should get you moving in the right direction.

2. Are you holding onto grievances, waiting for just the right time to demand an eye for an eye or pain for pain? If you are, what are you going to do with that pain, hurt, and frustration?

3. What holds you back from forgiving others? Why is this so hard?

4. What is the hardest part of receiving forgiveness?

5. Consider your life. Is it marked by forgiveness or by withholding forgiveness? What action, though difficult, might you need to pursue?

REACHING HIGHER

You probably know what I am about to say, and I don't say it lightly. Though there is nothing easy about what must be done, it is necessary. Perhaps you carry pain that cuts deep to the core of who you are. Every day, you bear the burden of what you have done to someone else or what someone else has done to you.

If you are the offender: seek forgiveness, knowing the Lord will forgive you and remove what you have done "as far as the east is from the west" (Ps. 103:12). I can't guarantee the response of the individual. However, as we have just talked about, the response is not for you to decide.

If you have been offended against, may you find it in your heart to forgive the person who harmed you. If you have the courage to tell him or her, let that person know you no longer hold what he or she said or did against that person. While there is nothing easy about this, it is good and will be freeing to your soul!

"Bored people are easy targets of the flesh and the Devil. It is like putting a bull's-eye on your chest with a sign: 'Tempt me. I'm easy!' Why? Because boredom is contrary to the natural, God-given impulse for fascination, excitement, pleasure, and exhilaration."

—*Sam Storm*[1]

12

ENTERTAIN ME—NOW!

GUIDEPOSTS

✴ You are growing up in a stimulating world that wants you to be dissatisfied.

✴ Pursuing a fast-paced life can desensitize you to both the beauty and suffering in creation.

✴ Boredom can lead to dangerous or devastating counterfeit adventures.

"I'M SO BORED" is one of the most dangerous sentences you can speak, and you have probably said it many, many times. If someone ever asked you why you were bored, you may have told him there was nothing to do. Was that really the answer? Or could it be that you had, maybe unknowingly, bought into our culture's sense of entitlement that screams, "Entertain me!"?

When my own three sons say they're bored, the problem seems to come from having too much to do, not too little. We want life to be fast-paced, unpredictable, instantaneous! Slow and predictable equals boring and meaningless. Think of the messages all around us: buy now, pay later, do it now, don't wait, ready in seconds, buy now for overnight shipping, available for a limited time only.

We do everything in a rush. If you're like me, when you stand in a ten-items-or-fewer line, you count the items in the cart in front of you. Doesn't it burn you when you discover the person ahead of you has twelve items? We have speedy lubes for our automobiles, apps for nearly everything we can imagine, creatine shakes to help us to bulk up to the body shape we want, one-week diets for losing fifteen pounds right away—guaranteed. A heartburn remedy that brings relief in thirty minutes is replaced by one that can do it in fifteen minutes. Millions believe an energy drink is a "win in a can." . . . The list can go on and on.

A DEADLY DISEASE

You might agree this is the reality we live in but wonder why we need to talk about it. It is vital to recognize the long-term effects your culture will have on you as you grow to manhood. If you desire the newest, biggest, and best, you will find yourself in a vicious cycle of never, never being satisfied.

Society begs to empty our wallets. It tells you your buddy down the street has something you want. The goal of advertising is to create dissatisfaction. That is why some thirty-second commercial spots during the 2012 Super Bowl cost over $5 million. $3.5 million of that covers air-time alone. Can you imagine paying $3.5 million for air—and for what purpose?[2] These commercials are aimed at the hearts of men and are anticipated almost as much as the game itself. Their goal is to make you so unsatisfied and bored with what you currently have that you feel compelled to buy, buy, buy. And if the advertising craze did not work, companies would not continue to throw such enormous amounts of money at an advertising blitz.

The book of Ecclesiastes traces how the wealthiest man in the world, Solomon, refused himself no pleasure and delighted in his work—but in the end lamented that all of it was as meaningless as chasing after the wind (cf. Eccles. 2:11). When our desire for more, bigger, and better intensifies, it has the opposite of its intended outcome: we become bored.

How so? Stimulation comes at us from every side. Eventually, we cannot react with much intensity to anything anymore, and atrophy sets in to the muscle of our imagination. In addition, when so much information and stimulation is fired at us, we have trouble sorting out what is important, relevant, and meaningful. Ordinary life becomes increasingly boring. We grow more dissatisfied. Like a drug addict, we want the next jolt or a bigger fix next time.

Boredom will bind your sense of contentment and chain you to a life of dissatisfaction subsidized by credit. It may, for example, result in a marriage that crashes and burns because your dark side of adventure leads you to an adulteress "with persuasive words" (Prov. 7:21). It will also force you to eventually retreat from the extremes of involvement. Let's take school as an example. If a math problem is too hard, or the life skills required for maturity take too long to develop, or we need discipline to do something painful, our first response is to avoid those slight discomforts at all costs. In our desire for lightning-fast speed, we may unknowingly create an appetite for stimulation that renders normal life very dull. The resulting attitude says, "We already know, we don't need this course, we don't need these dumb requirements, we don't need to read these antiquated books, attend this chapel, look at this painting, listen to this teacher, listen to my boss . . ."

WONDER WHERE WONDER WENT?

By this point, goodness and beauty seem so boring and unstimulating to many young men that they have lost their appreciation for art, a beautiful piece of music, a lone violin, a poem, the rolling thunder in the distance, the crack of lightning, the sound of birdsong, water rushing over rocks, majestic mountain views, or even silence.

Max Picard writes, "There is an immeasurability in happiness that only feels at home in the breadth of silence. Happiness and silence belong together just as do profit and noise."[3] Silence is always there, always listening and speaking. Too often, we think silence is empty. Have you ever considered sitting under a tree or perching on a rock looking over a canyon or across a mountain range—and being silent? If you find yourself in such a place for a period of time, you will learn the fullness of silence. Listen! What do you hear? What do you hear about you? What do you hear within you? What might God be speaking to you, about you, for you?

Sadly, boredom says the opposite. Boredom says silence is empty and must be filled. As a result, we are robbed of our sense of wonder; we lose it in our meaningless busyness. Before long, we become indifferent because we are bored and bored because we are indifferent. Man, you are meant for so much more than this. Stop and listen!

Regardless of where you live, you can choose to be bored or to be filled with awe and wonder. Don't make excuses. It doesn't matter if you live in the city and can't get to the mountains or the ocean or a place of peace and serenity. Refuse to run in the rat race. Simply be still. After all, the Lord says, "Be still, and know that I am God" (Ps. 46:10).

As you move toward manhood, you will have to approach this area with great deliberateness. When it comes to how you spend your time, you can either be a reactor or an initiator. Plan to cultivate your sense of wonder. If not addressed, boredom intensifies to the point where it not only stops us from being moved by the beautiful and the good, but it also takes away our eyes to see and to engage with the ugliness and the brokenness of life which screams for redemption—the entreaty God answered when he sent his Son to earth.

MISSING THE OBVIOUS

When we live a life focused on self, we become unable to see the very things that break the heart of Jesus. We become so absorbed in getting more and making ourselves look good that we cannot see the hurting, the broken, the poor, or the struggling neighbor. It's been said the true measure of a man is how he treats someone who can do him no good. Can you give, expecting absolutely nothing in return? Are you willing to engage instead of watch, to act instead of being passive?

Last week, my wife taught my sons this valuable lesson. As she stopped at a convenience store to put gas in the car, an old homeless man asked her for a hot dog. "No problem," she told him. Once they were inside the store, she asked him if he wanted two hot dogs and a soft drink and chips. After she paid for the food, the man asked her if she would take him to the homeless shelter. She told him to wait right there; she would come back after she checked with me.

My wife drove to my work to ask me about it. I immediately went into protector mode, rationalizing why this was not a good idea. However, as I looked into her eyes, I saw them well up with tears. My wife explained she had been asking God to bring someone into her path whom she might serve, who had nothing to directly offer or benefit her. She was overwhelmed at how God had answered her prayer.

Since I had to lead a meeting, I was not able to jump in the car, but another friend did. As my wife drove the man across town, my sons saw a real-life example of their mother seeing with the eyes of Jesus and serving as his hands and feet. When the man got out of the car and asked if she had fifty cents, Josiah quickly said, "I do," and handed the man the money. What a lesson she taught my boys that day!

Sadly, when we frantically try to fix our state of boredom, we can't even see the obvious—that we are the ones with the greatest need. We often say, "I will find my true joy and true satisfaction in those things that make me feel happy for the moment."

My most vivid personal example was when one of my life mentors decided to leave his wife and his children for another woman. After investing more than twenty-five years in that marriage, he decided to check out. I was devastated. How could this be? The man had been like a father to me. He believed in me; I trusted him. When a mutual friend asked him about the affair, he stated, "I know God wants me to be happy." *You have absolutely lost your mind!* I thought.

How can someone who was a trailblazer in so many ways get so far off the right path? My mentor wanted something he thought would be new and exciting and adventurous. In the process, he was willing to throw away everything that mattered for a few fleeting cheap thrills.

DAILY DELIGHT

What about God? How does he respond to this? Is God sitting back, feeling bored with his creation? He sure seemed pleased with the world when he made it. How does he feel after day after day after day of watching his creation work?

G. K. Chesterton beautifully considers the possible monotony of God's daily task:

> Children always say, "Do it again," and the grown-up person does it again until he is nearly dead. It is possible that God says every morning, "Do it again," to the sun and every evening, "Do it again," to the moon. It may not be automatic necessity that makes all the daisies alike. It may be that God makes every daisy separately but has never gotten tired of making them. It may be that He has an eternal appetite for infancy, for we have sinned and grown old and our Father is younger than we.[4]

This brings us back to the beginning of this book where I challenged you to get out of the house, to be like Frodo and leave the Shire for a much greater adventure. Let's not lose sight of the big picture. While some tasks may appear repetitive or monotonous, when we recognize we are called into the service of the Great King, these things take on a whole new meaning and purpose. We have a reason to pursue them with all the vigor and passion we can muster as we journey on!

DISCUSSION QUESTIONS

1. On a scale of 1–10 (1 being *poor* and 10 being *excellent*), how would you rate your level of contentment? Support your rating. What is it based on?

2. What is the byproduct of a life marked by discontentment and boredom? Based on what you have read, as well as your observations and experiences, how can discontentment and boredom be extremely dangerous?

3. To truly address discontentment and boredom, why must you shift your focus away from yourself?

4. With sustained success in this area, how might either your lifestyle or life pursuits change? (Consider your time, talents, treasures, and desires.)

REACHING HIGHER

God gives us the time we have. A year contains twelve months, fifty-two weeks, 365 days, 8,760 hours, 525,600 minutes, and 31,536,000 seconds (unless we are in a leap year). Each second is a gift from God. We have done nothing to deserve it, earn it, or purchase it. Each of us has the same twenty-four hours in a day. We can do nothing to stop time, slow it down, turn it off, or otherwise adjust it. Time marches on.

Past moments can be treasured or regretted but never lived again. We cannot bring back time. Moses understood this when he wrote, "Teach us to number our days aright that we may gain a heart of wisdom" (Ps. 90:12). In other words, make your few passing moments in this life count!

Anytime we say yes to something, we say no to something else. Plan deliberate time when you can listen to silence. (I'm going to go out on a limb and say that few have said yes to this very often.) This might sound like an odd next step to take in your journey, but when was the last time you spent any significant period of time in silence? At the end of chapter 7, I challenged you to get unplugged. That may be a prerequisite for pursuing this challenge.

Silence is not empty, nor is it boring. If you find it so, you simply grew impatient. As time passes, much will be said! Engage in the silence as you listen and record what you heard. What conversation are you having with God? What might he be communicating with you, to you, for you? As you dialogue with God, you may learn the next steps you are to take.

"A wise man is full of strength,
and a man of knowledge enhances his might,
for by wise guidance you can wage your war,
and in abundance of counselors there is victory.

—*Proverbs 24:5–6 (ESV)*

FLAMING DARTS

- ✳ You can overcome temptations through the power of Christ.
- ✳ As a son of the Great King, know that attacks from Satan are imminent!
- ✳ Satan uses sexual temptation as a primary tool to hinder good journey progress.
- ✳ Take heart, the ultimate battle has already been won by our Captain and King! *We win!*

OUR CONVERSATION on boredom and contentment becomes even more relevant when we talk about temptations. Before we dig into this essential issue, however, let's get a few things straight. When we talk about heart-level issues such as pride, discontentment. and temptation, we focus on the dark side of our hearts. We must find the correct perspective, or else we'll end up believing our hearts are utterly corrupt and unsalvageable. If we only look at verses such as Jeremiah 17:9, "The heart is deceitful above all things, and desperately sick" (ESV) or Matthew 15:19, "For out of the heart come evil thoughts," we will never be able to stand against the arrows of the Devil.

Why is that? We will give in, believing we cannot withstand the snares and temptations the Enemy puts in front of us. We will fail to see that, in Christ, we do have strength, and we can overcome the traitor within us. Don't be a sucker to defeatist thinking. Instead, take this encouragement from 1 Thessalonians 5:5–6:

> You are all sons of the light and sons of the day. We do not belong to the night or to the darkness. So then, let us not be like others, who are asleep, but let us be alert and self-controlled.

WHICH SIDE?

If you are a child of the great King Jesus, let's start by putting this in perspective. Puritan preacher and author Thomas Watson once said, "Satan doth not tempt God's children because they have sin in them, but because they have grace in them. Had they no grace, the devil would not disturb them."[1] Satan goes where the battle opposition is the strongest. He wants to strike the front lines, attacking the fiercest in battle, trying to take out the strongest and the bravest. If you are not under spiritual attack, you ought to be asking why not.

In 1655, Puritan William Gurnall wrote,

> A war between the Saint and Satan [is] so bloody a one, that the cruellest which was ever fought by men, will be found but sport and child's play to this. . . . The stage whereon this war is fought, is every man's own soul. [There] is no [neutral] in this war, the whole world is engaged in the quarrel, either for God against Satan, or for Satan against God.[2]

With these words, Gurnall strikes down the notion of neutrality, passivity, or refusal to engage in the battle. Theologian Cornelius Van Til adds clarity when he says,

172

There is not a square inch of ground in heaven or on earth or under the earth in which there is peace between Christ and Satan. . . . No one can stand back, refusing to be involved. . . . Jesus said, "He that is not with me is against me, and he that gathereth not with me scattereth abroad." If you say that you are "not involved" you are in fact involved on Satan's side.[3]

Are you getting the picture? This is a serious battle engagement. There are no conscientious objectors and no draft dodgers. You are in this war whether you like it or not. The question is—which side are you on?

DANGEROUS TERRAIN

When you step into the King's service, you become a marked man. The Enemy is certain; the target is you. You're at war, so you should expect conflict. Think of Frodo on his journey to destroy the ring. He ran up against a huge amount of conflict and adversity. It is no different for you. This is not the part of the journey where we see Frodo and Sam happily walking through the meadows as they leave the Shire. Our journey is taking us to an elevation where the air thins and the tree line recedes, leaving us more exposed and vulnerable to the elements.

Let me give you some startling statistics compiled by Dr. Richard J. Krejcir from surveys by Barna, Focus on the Family, and Fuller Seminary. His research sadly illustrates the point I have made about the focus and intentionality of the Devil's attacks, particularly against those in leadership.

Based on the research:

- "Fifteen hundred pastors leave the ministry each month due to moral failure, spiritual burnout, or contention in their churches.

173

- "Fifty percent of pastors' marriages will end in divorce.
- "Eighty percent of pastors feel unqualified and discouraged in their role as pastor.
- "Fifty percent of pastors are so discouraged that they would leave the ministry if they could, but have no other way of making a living.
- "Eighty percent of seminary and Bible school graduates who enter the ministry will leave the ministry within the first five years.
- "Seventy percent of pastors constantly fight depression."[4]

Stop right there! Maybe you are thinking, "Oh great, if the pastors across America can't stand up against the Devil's schemes, what hope do I have?" As long as pastors are your standard, you frankly have little chance of standing firm against the Enemy. Pastors are fallen, broken, and tempted sinners who regularly come under attack. They are not the standard.

John Owens said, "This steadfastness in believing doth not exclude all temptations from without. When we say a tree is firmly rooted, we do not say that the wind never blows upon it. The house that is built on the rock, is not free from assaults and storms."[5] Attack is imminent!

UNDER ATTACK

By this point in your life, most of you have had the flaming arrows of the Devil hurled at you. These arrows often bombard the mind with thoughts, impressions, and impulses contrary to God's word. Satan can unleash an unholy firestorm of arrows that essentially speak to you in such ways as this:

- Fear: "You have good reason to be afraid—now and always."

174

- Doubt: "You can't trust God."
- Lust: "You need to have your needs met . . . and this is how . . ."
- Jealousy: "Someone else is getting what you deserve."
- Guilt: "God will never forgive you."
- Greed: "You should have it! You deserve it! You need it! Go get it!"
- Unforgiveness: "You can never forgive that sin. Why would you even *want* to forgive him after he hurt you?"
- Anger: "You've been hurt and have a right to be mad."
- Discouragement: "You will never have your heart's desire."
- Pride: "You're above all that. You'd never stoop to that level."

While we are susceptible to any and all of these temptations, let's be sure we understand what temptations are all about. D. L. Moody said, "When Christians find themselves exposed to temptation they should pray to God to uphold them, and when they are tempted they should not be discouraged. It is not a sin to be tempted; the sin is to fall into temptation."[6] Jesus was repeatedly tempted, but he was sinless (Matt. 4; Heb. 2:17–18; 4:14). Sam Storms said, "Temptation only becomes a sin when you acquiesce to it, as it were 'fondle' it, and 'enjoy' it."[7]

SIMPLE BUT DEADLY

In chapter 5, I described in detail how the Devil dresses up sin, making it attractive to you. He tailors temptations for you that hit or prey on your weaknesses. While I won't repeat all that, the following two illustrations may make this point more clear.

175

Imagine your heart is like an apple the Devil wants to slice to the core. To do so, he does not come at you with a butcher knife. The cut would be so deep and the pain so intense that you would recoil in complete and utter shock. Instead, he comes at you with a plastic butter knife. At most, your skin is bruised. However, once that bruise goes away, the Devil comes back with a table knife. This time, he makes a cut, but it is superficial, and you know it will heal before long.

As time progresses, the Devil makes cut after cut. His blades get longer and sharper, the cuts become deeper, and the wound lasts longer. Before long, you have been run through with a wicked blade, yet you hardly felt the cold steel as it plunged deep into your heart. You have completely fallen to the temptation. You are left with the collateral damage, trying to figure out how everything went so wrong and how you can pick up the pieces.

The Enemy's strategy is simple. Imagine him as a rock climber trying to scale a canyon wall to claim territory on higher ground. As he begins to ascend from the canyon floor, he hopes for secure footing. However, he will be satisfied to make even very small gains at first. Even a toehold in the ascent will do. He will linger, barely hanging on, but still very much in pursuit of your heart. He will reposition his feet until he has a firm foothold. Once he achieves that, he will make haste to scale the canyon wall. Before long, he will pull himself to the top to declare his victory. He will reinforce his stronghold and claim that conquered territory (this area in your life) for his own. You have fallen.

Thomas Watson offers strong counsel for us when he says,

Do not enter into a dispute with Satan. When Eve began to argue the case with the serpent, the serpent was too hard for her; the devil, by his logic, disputed her out of paradise. Satan can mince sin, make it small, and garnish it over, and make it look like virtue. He is too subtle a sophister for us to hold an argument with him. Dispute not, but fight.[8]

DANGEROUS DESIRE

How is this relevant to your life? If you are honest with yourself, your mind is likely drawn to pornography. At this moment, you may be feeling guilt, shame, or remorse about it. Know there are millions around you experiencing the very same thing. Pornography is likely the greatest temptation in almost all young men's lives.

Can you remember back to when you first gave the Devil that toehold? Billy Sunday once said, "Temptation is the devil looking through the keyhole. Yielding is opening the door and inviting him in."[9] You might not want to admit you answered the door when the Devil knocked; perhaps you simply left the door wide open instead.

Remember God's words in Genesis 4:7: "Sin is crouching at your door; it desires to have you, but you must master it." When the sin is an issue of pornography or other sexual sins, everything becomes amplified. John Piper reminds us, "When sexual desire rises, Satan shifts his missile carriers into high gear. The rise of sexual desire does not mean victory for Satan, but does mean vulnerability to Satan."[10] First Corinthians 6:18 says, "Flee from sexual immorality. All other sins a man commits are outside his body, but he who sins sexually sins against his own body."

I love the words of Charles Brent, who said, "Only he who flings himself upward when the pull comes to drag him down, can hope to break the force of temptation. Temptation may be an invitation to hell, but much more is it an opportunity to reach heaven."[11] In one way, temptations are good in that they reveal what is in our hearts. Once we resist the temptation and secure our footing, sin also is avoided.

STRONG IN THE LORD

Although you currently might feel like "a man without self-control [who] is like a city broken into and left without walls" (Prov. 25:28 ESV), hear me when I say there is hope. God's grace, forgiveness, and healing are freely offered to you. Hear not just the words but the broken heart and humble pleading of David as he comes before God:

> Have mercy on me, O God,
>   according to your unfailing love;
> according to your great compassion
>   blot out my transgressions.
> Wash away all my iniquity
>   and cleanse me from my sin.
> For I know my transgressions,
>   and my sin is always before me.
> . . . .
> Cleanse me with hyssop, and I will be clean;
>   wash me, and I will be whiter than snow.
> Let me hear joy and gladness.
> . . . .
> Hide your face from my sins
>   and blot out all my iniquity.
> Create in me a pure heart, O God,
>   and renew a steadfast spirit within me.
> Do not cast me from your presence
>   or take your Holy Spirit from me.
> Restore to me the joy of your salvation
>   and grant me a willing spirit, to sustain me.
>   (Ps. 51: 1–3, 7–12)

An important question is asked and answered:

> How can a young man keep his way pure?
>> By living according to your word.
> I seek you with all my heart;
>> do not let me stray from your commands.
> I have hidden your word in my heart,
>> that I might not sin against you. (Ps. 119:9–11)

Moments of doubt and weakness are sure to arise. Prayer and accountability will serve you well at those times. Also, read and memorize God's word to encourage your own heart, rebuke the Devil, and call on God. As you go forward in your journey, allow the words of Scripture to lift your spirit, quicken your step, and revive your soul. These words are for you!

> Be strong, and show yourself a man, and keep the charge of the LORD your God, walking in his ways and keeping his statues, his commandments, his rules, and his testimonies . . . that you may prosper in all that you do and wherever you turn. (1 Kings 2:2–3 ESV)

> Be on your guard; stand firm in the faith; be men of courage; be strong. (1 Cor. 16:13)

> Finally, be strong in the Lord and in his mighty power. (Eph. 6:10)

When you have succumbed to the Great Traitor, and he has laid claim to areas of your life and heart, I urge you to not resign yourself to the fact. Reclaim that territory in the name of the King! The battle will be fierce as you war against the Great Deceiver and your own flesh. Yet fight you must! Fight the good fight in the name of our Captain and King, for our fiercest adversary will be forced to retreat at the name of Jesus.

You have that promise. Now claim that victory as you continue your journey!

DISCUSSION QUESTIONS

1. Identify the greatest area of temptation in your life. You must identify this to know where Satan will wage war. (Answer questions 2–4 with the answer to this question in mind.)

2. When does this temptation most often come?

3. When do you most easily give in and fall?

4. When have you been able to resist?

5. Identify where the Enemy has invaded and claimed territory in your life for his own. (This answer may be different from your answer to question 1.)

6. Do you want to take back this Enemy-claimed territory? If yes, then seek accountability from an older brother. If you have victory in this area of temptation, then claim it, declare it, and share it. You will find strength and courage to continue to fight the good fight.

REACHING HIGHER

Arm yourself with God's word. Commit some of the Scripture passages from this chapter to memory. Jesus showed us how to turn back the Devil when he quoted Scripture in the face of temptation. He knew the Devil could not stand up against God's word.

All the Scripture passages are good. However, I strongly encourage you to consider this one, which I mentioned in chapter 5:

> So, if you think you are standing firm, be careful that you don't fall! No temptation has overtaken you except what is common to man. And God is faithful; he will not let you be tempted beyond what you can bear. But when you are tempted, he will also provide a way out so that you can stand up under it. (1 Cor. 10:12–13)

I can't tell you how many times I have used this verse. You will find it helpful, so keep it close! Commit it to memory.

"There are three things that are too amazing for me,
four things that I do not understand:
the way of an eagle in the sky,
the way of a snake on a rock,
the way of a ship on the high seas,
and the way of a man with a maiden."

—*Proverbs 30:18–19*

14

THE DAUGHTERS OF EVE

GUIDEPOSTS

* Your God-given masculine design is to actively lay down your life for another.
* Our nature tends toward passivity and fails to offer true strength.
* True masculinity is to deny yourself and sacrificially serve . . . to the death!

AT THE CONCLUSION of my second date with the woman who is now my wife, I knew I was going to marry her. I was in the second semester of my junior year when one of my soccer teammates set me up on a blind date. It was a somewhat unusual situation since we both share the same first name and middle initial (which, by the way, made reciting our wedding vows rather interesting).

After our first meeting at a college basketball game, I followed up with an invitation to go out again. I was very much looking forward to the evening. I planned to pick Shawn up in my red Firebird before taking her to dinner and a concert.

The outing did not turn out quite as I had expected. That afternoon, I realized I was having car trouble and desperately

183

needed to find another vehicle. My best friend offered me his parents' van. Of course, that was a last resort, but it was my only option. What a horrible first impression this made when I picked Shawn up. I believe it was the van that made her mother a skeptic right from the start.

Shawn got into the van and off we drove on our first real date. A combination of being nervous in the presence of such beauty and not being used to a larger vehicle caused me to almost knock a pedestrian off the bridge and into the Allegheny River as the huge side mirrors just about sideswiped him. While parallel parking, I backed into the car behind me.

All in all, however, it was a great night. I walked back to my dorm room and told my buddies, "Someday I am going to marry that girl!" (I just needed to convince her it was a good idea!)

I wish I could tell you that dating that leads to marriage is just that easy. However, if I tried to convince you of this, I likely would lose all credibility.

A DIFFERENT DESIGN

When it comes to pursuing one of "Eve's daughters," nothing will make your heart beat faster, make you feel more alive, and cause you to feel your strength more than when you are in the presence of the captivating girl who has won your heart. Simultaneously, nothing is more risky and more unnerving, because the differences between guys and girls are vast and sometimes can be confusing to figure out. Yet understanding these differences will save you from making many assumptions, drawing conclusions, and reacting in a way that will foul up your relationship with a young woman.

Looking back at dating and at the past nineteen years of marriage, I have found plenty of instances where I failed to take into consideration the beautiful and wonderful ways in which my wife is designed differently from myself.

Gary Smalley provides a wonderful analogy of the differences between men and women by comparing a butterfly and a buffalo.

> The butterfly has a keen sensitivity. It is sensitive to the slightest breeze. . . . It notices the beauty of even the tiniest of flowers. Because of its sensitivity, it is constantly aware of all the changes going on around it and is able to react to the slightest variation in its environment. Thus, the butterfly reacts with swiftness toward anything that might hurt it.[1]

While this is a powerful portrayal of the feminine side, equally graphic is the description of the buffalo:

> The buffalo is another story. It is rough and calloused. It doesn't react to a breeze. It's not even affected by a thirty-mile-an-hour wind. It just goes right on doing whatever it was doing. It's not aware of the smallest of flowers, nor does it appear to be sensitive to slight changes in its environment. . . . The buffalo isn't "rotten to the core" just because he goes around stepping on pretty flowers. In fact, the buffalo's toughness is an extreme asset. His strength, when harnessed, can pull a plow that four grown men can't pull. . . . [The man] may plow through circumstances, while [the woman} may "feel" life and [her] surroundings with much more sensitivity.[2]

Of course, while this comparison can be helpful, let me be quick to say that I have often seen some of these traits displayed in the opposite sex. For example, when one of my sisters came home from the army, she could do seventy real push-ups in sixty seconds. No kidding! Conversely, my college roommate and lifelong friend says he cries at the opening of a new Wal-Mart store as a way to illustrate that he can be rather sentimental!

Still, it's important for you to understand that God has designed you with the capacity to accomplish amazing feats with strength and power and fortitude when the winds of life are blowing. You can stand tall and firm like an oak tree and press through the fiercest of storms, the most intense battles . . . and come out on the other side victorious. This is a great thing!

There is, however, a time and a place to use these traits. Applying them unilaterally, without considering the excellent characteristics of the "daughters of Eve," can have damaging effects on your relationship and can cause real harm to girls. The Creator of all things designed man and woman with great care. He intended the differences between men and women to be pleasurable, delightful, complementary, and enjoyed. Too many times, I have been in "buffalo-mode" and have awkwardly stomped through relational life-circumstances with little regard to the fact that I was not dealing with another buffalo but with my wife, who, much like a butterfly, deserves to be treated with the utmost kindness, care, and gentleness.

THE SIN OF ADAM

As we consider the differences between girls and guys, we can talk about so many different things. However, I would like to focus on several specific areas directly applicable to you. The first point, which I raised in chapter 7, concerns Adam's passivity while Eve ate the fruit. Whenever I am in a youth group/conference and this matter comes up, the guys get rowdy and high-five each other, pointing at the girls when the speaker talks about how all mankind fell by Eve's sin.

When you look at Scripture, this is exactly what it says: "When the woman saw that the fruit of the tree was good for food and pleasing to the eye, and also desirable for gaining wisdom, she took some and ate it. She also gave some to her husband, who was with her, and he ate it" (Gen. 3:6). Guys, now is the time to stop the cheering. Notice two words about Adam's position in the garden. The author says Adam was "with her."

Could it be that Eve was alone and related this incident to Adam after she ate? If Eve had eaten the fruit, come to Adam, and offered him some, don't you think he would have been shocked? He might have asked, "You did *what?* God said not to eat of that tree! How could you? What were you thinking?" No, I don't believe it happened that way. It seems likely that Adam and Eve had already considered eating the fruit before they actually did so. Considering temptations and how the Devil works, it would be surprising if the serpent came to Eve, convinced her and Adam to sin, and neither saw reason to object. The serpent was likely all they needed to convince themselves this was a good idea because they had been thinking about it for some time.

Not only was Adam right there with Eve, but his sin caused the blame and accountability for his actions to shift to him and to all mankind. In the New Testament, Paul credits Adam with this in Romans 5:12: "Therefore . . . sin entered the world through one man, and death through sin, and in this way death came to all men, because all sinned." Spiritual death or separation from God is due to Adam's act.

When Adam passively stood by as the greatest temptation known to mankind went down, he failed to understand his place and his role. God had placed him in Eden to be a caretaker of the Garden. He was not to usurp God's authority or commands, nor was he to lord his authority over Eve. He was to be submissive to God and to care for Eve and the garden, as God had commissioned him to do in Genesis 2:15–16. He was to be both a gardener and guardian.

After he sinned, God called Adam out. His response is telling of his new and fallen nature. In Genesis 3:10, Adam tells God that he was afraid, naked, and hiding. Those three words alone ought to throw up a red flag and stop us in our tracks. However, self-absorbed Adam could only find it in himself to blame his problems on Eve instead of repentantly responding to God's voice.

TAKE RESPONSIBILITY

So where does that leave us? Are we as guys supposed to throw up our hands and say, "Well, if he couldn't stand for what is right, how can I ever do it?" Absolutely not! To think that is to minimize the power of Christ to work in and through you to do his will and his work.

So what is our role?

Simply put (yet difficult in practice), we are to take responsibility for our actions. After all, although Adam and Eve both sinned, Adam was the one whom God first held responsible for the sin. Genesis 3:9 reads, "And God called out *to the man* . . ." Like Adam, too often our passivity and our defensiveness collide, and strength in humility and sincere repentance are quickly buried underground. If there is an area where most young men do not want the strength of true godliness to emerge, it is in the area of physical relationships with their girlfriends.

During a recent counseling session with a teenage couple, I discussed their PDA (public displays of affection). As the conversation developed, I had to stop and tell the young man that the primary issue was no longer PDA but his defensive response. He was full of excuses and blame-shifting. He brought up what others were doing, wanted to know who else had been talked to, asked why he and his girlfriend were being singled out, and tried to tell me that what they were doing was not that bad. When I asked if the points I'd raised were valid, he said, "Not really."

At that, his girlfriend interrupted him and said, "What he is saying is legit. We need to cool it and quit acting so immature."

Whoa! Up to this point, the young man had been leading— but not in the right direction. He had failed to stop, take inventory, assume responsibility, and address where he was wrong. When "Eve" stepped forward and said what she did, the conversation went in a completely different direction.

I found it interesting that even in front of me the girl-friend was willing to say their PDA was too much and needed to stop. Why didn't the young man arrive at this conclusion on his own? Up to that point, all his answers were defensive. He was thinking only about himself instead of what was right and what was the best way to serve, guard, and care for his girlfriend. However, this is not surprising.

In a "hook-up" world where sex is supposed to involve no commitments, no strings attached, no real emotions, no standards, and no convictions, our tendency is to look at girls as "friends with benefits." That phrase alone suggests a self-ish attitude that only considers how the relationship might benefit and satisfy self. The end result of this way of thinking can often be "casual" sex.

Casual sex, however, is anything but casual. In *The Screwtape Letters*, C. S. Lewis explains it this way: "The truth is that wherever a man lies with a woman, there, whether they like it or not, a transcendental relation is set up between them which must be eternally enjoyed or endured."[3] A study in 2000 indicated that 55 percent of all teenage boys who had sex wished they had waited longer (72 percent of the girls regretted their choice).[4]

189

The Russian author Fyodor Dostoyevsky offers us a warning when he says, "Beauty is not only a terrible thing, it is also a mysterious thing. There God and the Devil strive for mastery, and the battleground is the heart of man."[5] Young men, do not let your hearts go passive. Be strong, unwavering, and hold to what you know is right and true. "Flee the evil desires of youth, and pursue righteousness, faith, love and peace, along with those who call on the Lord out of a pure heart" (2 Tim. 2:22).

THE SUITABLE HELPER

Let's flip from viewing girls as an object "designed to benefit me" to the more healthy perspective we encounter very early in Scripture. In Genesis 2:18, God uses a valuable word to describe Eve when he says, "It is not good for man to be alone. I will make a helper suitable for him."

We must be careful how we look at the word "helper." Taken to one extreme, this word could suggest that man is helpless and desperately incompetent. Yet the other extreme could suggest that the guy is always in the lead and that the woman is to stay behind him, following orders, helping where and when asked. Instead, "helper" is actually a majestic term! After all, God himself is described as an "ever-present help in trouble" (Ps. 46:1). The woman is a helper for men who need help.

I personally can vouch for how true this really is. What a mess I would be without my helpmate. My wife is not a clone or a duplicate of me. She is loving and nurturing; she has a spectacularly calming affect on our home and in our marriage. Adam's sons did not need another hunting or fishing buddy; instead, they needed a woman.

I've heard it said that the location of the bone God chose to use in creating Eve indicates where she belongs. God did not choose a bone from Adam's head or from his foot. Rather, he chose a rib from Adam's side . . . and that is where Eve belongs: side-by-side with Adam.

My wife has been an incredible helpmate for the nearly nineteen years we have been married. This does not mean she only does chores or runs errands. Rather, we are walking side by side through life together. We enjoy each other's company and enjoy simply living life together. On an even greater scale, I have watched my parents do the same for close to forty-five years. They are inseparable. Now in their early seventies, they are highly capable of going places and doing many things; however, they rarely go separate ways. They just love being with each other! It is a beautiful thing for my wife, my sons, and myself to see.

Right now, you might feel like the last thing you need is the help of a girl. Please hear me when I say you need more help than you realize. You may need to shift your thinking. Maybe, like me, you thought girls were icky through the first few grades of school. Then they became kind of cute to you, and you flirted with them through your middle school years. Then, high school rolled around, and they became almost a trophy. Maybe you think, "If only I could date that girl. Just think how my status would shoot through the roof!" Maybe you even base your personal worth and accomplishments on the type of girlfriend you think you can or maybe should "get." Aren't the quarterbacks of the football team or the star basketball players the ones who always date the pretty girls?

Recently, one of my midfielders ripped a left-footed shot from twenty-five yards out into the corner of the goal past the outstretched hand of the diving keeper. As players jogged back to get ready for the kickoff, one of the guys on the bench exclaimed, "Now Josh will be able to upgrade his girlfriend!"

As you can imagine, I turned around and said, "Have I taught you nothing?" The players who heard laughed hysterically.

It sounds ridiculous as I write these words—but don't guys too often view girls as a commodity to be gained or achieved? Instead of putting a trophy on your shelf, you seek a status symbol to drape about your arm. This is not only a narrow view but also a bad one: it not only overlooks God's design for women but also his design for male and female interaction and our way of being together. If you hold this view, it may be best to break up with your girlfriend until you get a lesser view of yourself and a greater view of her as a wonderful image-bearer of God.

LAY DOWN YOUR LIFE

God gives husbands a very serious command in Ephesians 5:25 when he says, "Husbands, love your wives, just as Christ loved the church and gave himself up for her." This instruction for husbands to love their wives as Christ loved the church should radically affect how a husband treats his wife. Yet even if you are not married, isn't this something you should be thinking about and putting into practice now?

First, we must ask ourselves exactly how Christ loved the church. He laid down his life for it. He emptied himself, gave up his glory, set aside his kingly rights, took on the form of a servant, and literally died for the church, his bride. What radical implications this has for a male-female relationship!

What does it mean to lay down our life for another? Doing so sounds like a major event that might require some planning. Wrong! This is an all-the-time thing. Laying down your life simply means putting someone else's life before your own. It means being last instead of first, going without so someone else can have, not thinking about yourself so much, and looking for ways to give while expecting nothing in return.

Sadly, today men can get a compliment for the slightest act of thoughtfulness, as if their kindness is a rarity to be treasured.

I wish I could say I am the greatest servant I know. Instead, this honor goes to my wife as she gives her time, attention, and energy to our family. I have work to do in this area!

While we are talking about laying down our lives for others, let me clarify something. The work you do in the occupation to which you have been/will be called is different from what I am proposing. You might be a great servant-leader in your sport, schoolwork, or job, but that is not what I am talking about. Too often, we find our identity in what we do.

SHOW SOME RESPECT

When was the last time that you did something for a girl, neither expecting nor taking anything in return? Think about this. This is important. If you are struggling to come up with an answer, this is a problem.

There comes a night that many girls dream about, likely only second to their wedding day in their minds, and that is prom! At our school, prom is in late April. However, I have seen our female students begin looking for prom dresses as early as January. Many will drop a couple hundred dollars or more for their perfect dress. This is a major, major event.

As guys, you have a wonderful opportunity in front of you. You can step forward to purchase the tickets for your date, secure the ride to the prom, set up reservations, pay for a great dinner, buy flowers, and rent a tux so you look presentable in her pictures. Throughout the entire night, you have the opportunity to show you respect her and have deliberately chosen to honor her as a young woman who is fearfully and wonderfully made in the image of God. If you really wrestle with this concept, it will direct how you dance, speak, and conduct yourself for the entirety of the evening.

Specifically, you will seize the opportunity to show your date and her parents that you value her and them by taking care of her in a God-honoring way right up to the point of having her home a bit earlier than the agreed-on time. (I'm telling you, this is a good tip.) As you drive away, be sure your conscience is clear and you did not take or even expect something from her that you had no business taking or expecting. In the morning, you will feel great to know you honored, respected, and treated her in this manner. Meanwhile, her appreciation and respect for you most likely will leap exponentially.

What I am suggesting is completely countercultural. A few nights ago, I sat with my teenage son and a few of his buddies as we watched Super Bowl XLVI. We turned off nearly every other commercial to avoid watching a woman's scantily clad body being used to sell some car or other product. I took the opportunity to tell the guys that we cannot support watching commercials that degrade women and reduce them to sex objects. God has a much higher and greater view of women and so must we.

FIGHTING THE GOOD FIGHT

Think back on what we have discussed regarding temptations and the need for prayer, accountability, and time meditating on God's word. This requires intentional time on a routine basis. Unfortunately, we have become accustomed to two-hour movies that always seem to involve a damsel in distress or conflict between the man and woman. Without fail, by the end of the movie, it all works out: the woman is saved, the man is the hero, every conflict is resolved, life is good, and they all live happily ever after. That is not real life!

If you are in a dating relationship, you have made some serious relational deposits. I encourage you to work on serving like Christ and achieving victory over the passivity of Adam.

John 15:13 says, "Greater love has no one than this, that he lay down his life for his friends."

> And this is my prayer: that your love may abound more and more in knowledge and depth of insight, so that you may be able to discern what is best and may be pure and blameless until the day of Christ. (Phil. 1:9–10)

Practically speaking, you may have found this chapter unnerving if you have fallen prey to the wrong thinking I described. Consider the next steps you need to take. As God convicts you of errors you have made, you may need to confess these faults and ask forgiveness. As the Lord has opened my eyes, I have had to ask forgiveness from my wife for things I have said or done . . . sometimes offenses from years ago. While it is never enjoyable to rehash painful moments from the past or to admit and confess your faults, this is a must if you ever expect true healing and restoration to take place.

Over the years, I have watched self-seeking guys who are in relationships only for themselves emotionally scar countless girls. While most would never admit that this attitude describes them, the evidence found in broken, locked-away hearts is convicting and sobering.

Men, we may never in this life know the power of our words and actions to affect the lives and hearts of those of the opposite sex. We have a responsibility to not only guard our own hearts but also to protect and care for the hearts of girls we know. We must cease being passive when the strength of our honor, character, integrity, dignity, respect, and virtue most desperately needs to emerge.

As we take our eyes off ourselves, we can begin to see with the relationally-transforming eyes of Jesus and properly serve the daughters of Eve.

DISCUSSION QUESTIONS

1. Do you ever find yourself becoming passive in your relationships with girls? If so, where and when? Some key areas to consider might be in decision-making or in being proactive in planning or setting boundaries for a dating relationship.

2. How has this chapter changed your way of thinking regarding men and women and their different God-given design? How might this alone change your interactions with the "daughters of Eve"?

3. In the New Testament, the apostle Paul puts the blame on Adam for the fall of mankind. What are the implications for all of Adam's sons, particularly in light of their relationships and interactions with girls?

4. How might you lay down your life for one of Eve's daughters? How can you serve while expecting nothing in return?

5. How might a growing relationship with Christ actually deepen your relationship with a young woman you are pursuing?

REACHING HIGHER

1. If dating, what specific boundaries have you and your girlfriend discussed and agreed to? If you have not discussed this, I strongly encourage you to consider setting boundaries. (If not dating, thinking over boundaries would still be a great exercise to complete.)

2. Have you shared these boundaries with a mentor in your life who can pray for you and help to hold you accountable? If not, whom might you share this with *today*?

3. In this chapter, we spoke of recognizing differences between girls and guys, standing for the truth, not being passive, serving others, and setting boundaries. While this has not been a driving theme in this specific chapter, I would challenge you to consider what role prayer and God's word has in your conversations and interactions with girls. This alone will shape and define (or redefine) your relationships in amazing ways.

PART 4

MOVING TOWARD THE SUMMIT

"The humblest [house], therefore, may produce you your greatest man. . . . That is the process of life, this constant surging up of the new strength of unnamed, unrecognized, uncatalogued men who are just getting into the running, who are just coming up from the masses of the unrecognized multitude. You do not know when you will see above the level masses of the crowd some great stature lifted head and shoulders above the rest, shouldering its way, not violently but gently, to the front and saying, 'Here am I; follow me.' And his voice will be your voice, his thought will be your thought, and you will follow him as if you were following the best things in yourselves."

—*Woodrow Wilson*[1]

AN INVITATION TO LEAD

GUIDEPOSTS

* You are a leader and an influence on the people around you.
* Leaving places of safety and security will be uncomfortable and unnerving.
* When you lead out of areas of weakness, the power of Christ becomes evident.

ABOUT TEN YEARS AGO, I was attending a conference while working on my doctorate in Scottsdale, Arizona. For the first several days, I eyed Camelback Mountain: the backdrop to the conference site. When given an afternoon off from classes, I asked a colleague if he would like to climb Camelback Mountain with me, and he readily agreed.

With the dry heat reaching around 115 degrees on that July mid-afternoon, we knew we needed to arm ourselves with bottles of water. As we eagerly set out, I realized the hike was going to take longer than I had anticipated. While I was well conditioned, my older colleague soon began to tire as we labored up the mountain.

By about halfway up, he had finished his entire water bottle and looked pale. I asked him if he wanted to stop and turn back, but he said he really wanted to get to the top.

Almost three fourths of the way up, he had drunk almost all my water as well. When I noticed he was no longer sweating, I put my foot down and said I did not think it would be good for him to go on. Now quick to agree, he said, "You go ahead to the top. I'll wait here for you."

Those words were all I needed. Life sprang into my legs, and I bounded to the top of the mountain to catch a glimpse of a most rewarding view.

LEADERSHIP IN A WORD

On our journey together, we have discussed many things to provide you with a foundation for the next major step in your life. Up to this point, you have been following behind. However, a time will come when you must assume the lead.

You might recall the story from chapter 3 in which my coach took the teams' flashlights and left us in the caves to find our own way in the dark. While we all knew our coach was still in the cave and we had not been simply left to our own devices to find our way out, we still felt a sense of responsibility, anxiety, and even fear. Those were normal and natural feelings. We felt responsible because the coach had trusted us enough to allow us to assume some leadership. Yet, we also felt great anxiety, because we truly were stepping into the unfamiliar and uncomfortable.

One of the great lessons I took from that event was not just the need for vocal leaders, but the importance of everyone involved. Each guy played a major role in finding Coach in that pitch-black cave. Although everyone was out of his comfort zone, each led in his own unique way. Some were the vocal leaders, others took the front and back of the line, others encouraged the two guys who were claustrophobic and terrified, and we all spoke to the guys in front and behind us as we felt for protruding rocks, water holes, and other obstacles around us. In other words, everyone had a vital role that he could and did fill.

When you step up like young Samuel in the Bible and say, "Here I am; I am ready to serve," you don't always know what the task entails and what it will require of you. However, we offer our lives as "living sacrifices" to be used as God sees fit (cf. Rom. 12:1).

When we speak of leadership, we often misunderstand what leadership involves. Some of you naturally run to the front, assuming a leadership position by "leading the charge." However, leadership can also be defined as *guidance*.[2] Just as my teammates and I guided each other in the dark caves, so you serve as a guide, and thus a leader, to the people around you.

How is that?

Simply put, it comes down to influence. You might not utter a word, yet your actions, attitude, and lifestyle communicate a message to those around you. That means every guy reading this book can be a leader! As you continue to read, consider your "sphere of influence" (those people you affect right now). Are you a good influence or a bad one?

I love to visit the elderly in a nursing home, an activity that might sound odd or even dull. However, the guidance those men and women give me is astonishing. As their lives draw to a close, they reflect on what has been most valuable and most disappointing and what they would do again if they had the chance. After receiving answers to my questions, I leave feeling like I've been given a new vision for my life, as if someone hit the reset or refresh button. Many offer a word of challenge or even admonishment, such as,

"Remember to love your wife" or "Value your time with your sons, because it will pass much too quickly!" That is influence; that is leadership!

EXAMPLES OF INFLUENTIAL LEADERS

Do not let your youth stand in your way. We see wonderful examples in the Bible of younger men taking the lead with vigor, passion, and enthusiasm. When God did not permit Moses to enter the Promised Land, Joshua emerged as the courageous leader of the Israelites. When God took Elijah to heaven in a chariot of fire, Elisha kept Elijah's cloak as a symbol of the leadership he was to assume. The apostle Paul, sensing his days in prison were drawing to a close and his death was near, gave deliberate instructions to Timothy telling him how he ought to preach and lead once he was gone. Just before his ascension into heaven, Jesus went to the mountains of Galilee and gave his eleven disciples the Great Commission.

In each case, the mentor spent significant time with the one(s) who would carry on his mission. Various translations use different words to denote the relationship between Moses and Joshua. However, in each case, the words *servant,* *assistant,* or *minister* clearly characterize these close mentoring relationships. Moses spent a considerable amount of time with Joshua—in fact, Joshua went up Mount Sinai with Moses to get the Ten Commandments. Elijah and Elisha had grown so close that when Elijah told him to stay put because God was calling Elijah away, Elisha responded three times by saying, "No, I will not leave you" (cf. 2 Kings 2:2). Before Elijah was taken by God, he asked Elisha what he could do for him. Elijah asked for a double portion of his spirit—not out of a desire to outdo Elijah but in order to be used by God as a strong leader for the weak nation of Israel. Paul was clear and direct in his instructions to Timothy as he writes,

> Preach the Word; be prepared in season and out of season; correct, rebuke and encourage—with great patience and careful instruction. For the time will come when men will not put up with sound doctrine. Instead, to suit their own desires, they will gather around them a great number of teachers to say what their itching ears want to hear. They will turn their ears away from the truth and turn aside to myths. But you, keep your head in all situations, endure hardship, do the work of an evangelist. (2 Tim. 4:2–5)

Finally, the resurrected Jesus, after teaching his disciples riveting lessons for three years and then laying down his life for his people, spoke some very empowering words to his disciples:

> All authority in heaven and on earth has been given to me. Therefore go. . . . And surely I am with you always, to the very end of the age. (Matt. 28:18–20)

INVITED TO LEAD

Paul instructed Timothy not to let others look down on him just because he was young (1 Tim. 4:12). He knew Timothy's age would be a stumbling block for some people; this was an obstacle Timothy would have to overcome. To do so, Timothy needed to live a blameless life that would show others how to honor and please God. He was to be an example to other believers as well as to the unsaved.

I'm sure Timothy felt intimidated and inadequate at times for the job he had been called to fill. A bit of self-doubt, however, is not too bad a thing. When you get overconfident, you can begin to think your abilities alone will get you through. The end result will be a valiant charge and a quick death. You can't depend just on yourself.

By God's grace, I have been somewhat ahead of the curve for much of my life. At the age of twenty-four, I was school principal. At twenty-nine, I received my doctorate degree and was the head of a school with 650 students. In my first year as middle school principal, one family was adamant: they were not going to send their middle school children to a school where the principal was only twenty-four years old. They meant it, and they stuck to their position.

A major reason I was able to assume those responsibilities at a young age was because I had a mentor who believed in me. I met with him regularly. He challenged me to get my master's degree and then mentored me through my first year as middle school principal.

In the same way, I was a varsity soccer coach my first year out of college. We won the state championship that first year, and people thought more highly of me than they should have. My college coach had prepared me for that moment. When I had been a senior captain in college, he had given me opportunities to take the college junior varsity team on away games and to actually coach them.

In each case, my mentors had in essence said, "You go on ahead. If you need help, I am willing and ready to help, but I believe you are ready!" The confidence those men had in me meant more than words can say. I am eternally grateful for their willingness to let me take risks and, at the same time, provide the support, encouragement, guidance, accountability, and feedback I needed to lead using the gifts God was developing in me. They gave me more than permission to lead—they gave me an invitation. They were some of the greatest leaders I know, because they were intent on positively affecting my attitude and behaviors.

COURAGE UNDER FIRE

Considering the times, the perspective on youth, and the weightiness of the gospel, Paul is very clear in his instructions to Titus. In Titus 2:6–8, Paul writes:

> Encourage the young men to be self-controlled. In everything set them an example by doing what is good. In your teaching show integrity, seriousness and soundness of speech that cannot be condemned, so that those who oppose you may be ashamed because they have nothing bad to say about us.

Why did Paul emphasize living a life that is above reproach? Because many people will be skeptical of your abilities, talents, and gifts. Some may even hope that you will fail in your position.

One of my favorite quotes comes from President Teddy Roosevelt's speech "Citizenship in a Republic." He declared:

> It is not the critic who counts; not the man who points out how the strong man stumbles, or where the doer of deeds could have done them better. The credit belongs to the man who is actually in the arena, whose face is marred by dust and sweat and blood; who strives valiantly; who errs, who comes up short again and again, because there is no effort without error or shortcoming; but who does actually strive to do the deeds; who knows great enthusiasms, the great devotions; who spends himself in a worthy cause; who at the best knows in the end the triumph of high achievement, and who at the worst, if he fails, at least fails while daring greatly, so that his place

207

shall never be with those cold and timid souls who neither know victory nor defeat.[3]

If you are one of those out-front leaders, know that the front of the pack can be very lonely at times. As you climb higher, the air grows thinner and breathing grows more difficult; you also stand out as an easy target for potshots and jabs. Yet, stick with it, man. Remember whom you are ultimately serving through your leadership. In Psalm 115:1, the psalmist writes, "Not to us, O LORD, not to us but to your name be the glory because of your love and faithfulness." When you unselfishly and humbly lead for the glory of God, you will be amazed at how people willingly listen and follow.

In 1914, President Woodrow Wilson gave a speech to the Christian Men's Association titled, "The Power of Christian Young Men." The following rich excerpt further illustrates this point.

> The only way your powers [influence or leadership] can become great is by exerting them outside the circle of your own narrow, special, selfish interests. And that is the reason of Christianity. Christ came into the world to save others, not to save himself; and no man is a true Christian who does not think constantly of how he can lift his brother, how he can assist his friend, how he can enlighten mankind, how he can make virtue the rule of conduct in the circle in which he lives. . . . Christian young men . . . [are] meant to put [their] shoulders under the world and lift it, so that other men may feel that they have companions in bearing the weight and heat of the day; that other men may know that there are those who care for them, who would go into places of difficulty and danger to rescue them, who regard themselves as their brother's keeper.[4]

In other words, a young leader needs to be self-sacrificing, hold strong convictions, and have a cause worth fighting and dying for.

PASSIONS + BURDENS + VISION = MISSION

How can you best discover how you should lead through your influence on those around you? Spend considerable time identifying your burdens and your passions. Your passions should be the things to which you are deeply committed. They make you want to get up in the morning or leave you lying awake dreaming about them. Our burdens are those things that break our hearts or bring us to tears.

As a shepherd boy, David was deeply committed to protecting his sheep, and then the Israelites, even at the potential expense of his own life. In Philippians 3:8, Paul wrote, "I consider everything a loss compared to the surpassing greatness of knowing Christ Jesus my Lord, for whose sake I have lost all things. I consider them rubbish, that I may gain Christ." In Philippians 1:20, Paul said his chief aim in life was magnifying Christ—in other words, to put Christ on display and make him look great! You can feel the passion explode from the pages of Scripture as you read Paul's words. Jesus was passionate about fulfilling his Father's mission to seek and save the lost and to redeem a people to himself through his work on the cross!

David was burdened by the loss of his friend Jonathan but was intent on caring for Jonathan's son as his own. David's heart broke over his own sin and the sin of his sons. His repentant and broken spirit is most evident in the vivid, heartrending words he used in the Psalms to describe his feelings of despair while wrestling with issues of sin and loneliness. Paul's heart was burdened to see the church and its people follow the teachings of Jesus. He was intent to lead and mentor men like Timothy so they would be prepared for the important role they needed to fill.

As we know, Jesus was deeply burdened by us! Throughout the New Testament, we see him feeling and showing

209

compassion toward a crowd or a single individual. We see him crying over the death of Lazarus and weeping as he looked over the city of Jerusalem, knowing his people had refused to listen to him.

When burdens and passions collide, you have found your specific, unique mission where you can, and probably should, seek to influence and lead others. Your mission might take you across the street to your neighbors; it might take you literally around the world.

When you live and lead out of your passions and burdens, something amazing happens. You feel blood rushing through your veins and your heart beating through your chest, and you know you are more alive than you can imagine. Not only that, but you find yourself used for a good and worthy cause that extends far beyond yourself.

THE DESCENT

I am not giving you a formula for success according to the world's standards. That formula says get more, hold on to what you have, get the next best thing on the market, and make safety and security your ultimate pursuit. As my pastor, Joe Novenson, recently said, "Sacrifice and service have been murdered by safety and security." A life in the safe zone isn't living . . . it's a life spent waiting around for death to do its thing.

No, I'm pointing you to another trailhead where the way is rugged and the descent more difficult. I say *descent* because this is what true leadership is all about: going down instead of up, serving instead of being served. Leadership is about the other and not about you. Leadership puts other lives before your own life. It gives instead of gets. It takes risks over safety. Jesus said, "Whoever loses their life for my sake will find it" (Matt. 10:39). Simply put, if you want to know what real living is all about, give your life away for the sake of the cross. Jim Elliot wrote in his journal, "He is no fool who gives what he cannot keep to gain that which he cannot lose."[5]

We see others around us living boldly for a cause greater than themselves. A man who comes to my mind is former star NFL player Pat Tillman. He turned down a $3.6 million contract with the Arizona Cardinals in order to join the U.S. Army in the war in Afghanistan. When people wondered at his decision, Tillman said, "Sports embodied many of the qualities I deem meaningful. However, these last few years, and especially after recent events, I've come to appreciate just how shallow and insignificant my role is. . . . It's no longer important."[6] In 2004, his decision cost him his life when he was shot three times in the head while protecting a fellow soldier.

I myself am most passionate and burdened to see my three sons walk with the Lord. I desire that for them more than anything else in the world. Similarly, I am deeply passionate about the topic I'm writing on. I want to play whatever part I can to bring young men to boldly follow Christ. I could go on and on about this, but the reality is I have already done just that. If you have read up to this point, you have a fair understanding of how my passions and burdens have collided to give way to my vision for young men.

Those who know of me might think my passion is coaching soccer. However, those who know me well know coaching soccer has something to do with the game but everything to do with helping to guide young men on their journey toward biblical manhood.

But what about you?

I can tell you firsthand that this path is not easy. However, take great strength and courage from the fact that the

Lord will give you the grace to stand, to lead, and to influence where you never thought possible. Second Chronicles 16:9 says, "For the eyes of the LORD range throughout the earth to strengthen those whose hearts are fully committed to him."

So I ask again, "What about *you?*"

Robert Frost concludes his poem, "The Road Not Taken," with the words:

> Two roads diverged in a wood, and I—
> I took the one less traveled by,
> And that has made all the difference.[7]

DISCUSSION QUESTIONS

1. What are your burdens as defined by this chapter?

2. What are your passions?

3. Where does your leadership and influence currently extend? (Identify whom you influence or lead and to what extent.)

4. As you consider your burdens and passions, what might God be calling you to do?

5. What are the areas of anxiety or worry that flood your mind when you think about how you might be called to lead? (It is good to identify them; just not to run as Jonah once did!)

6. With whom might you share what you believe God is calling you to do? (Remember that Moses felt completely inadequate, and God gave him Aaron to begin his first leadership steps. However, it was Moses who was given

the task to lead God's people.) Ask for help, but don't run or hide.

REACHING HIGHER

The Lord may be giving you a passionate heart moved by compassion. He may be giving you the vision to see what could be. He may be giving you the conviction of what *should* be.

Vision demands change; it implies movement. Vision requires someone to champion the cause. So I ask you not what *might* God be calling you to do, but what *will* you go and do?

Identify the steps to take—and then take the first one. *Go* . . . today!

"I am of the opinion that my life belongs to the whole community and as I live, it is my privilege—my priviledge to do for it what I can. I want to be thoroughly used up when I die, for the harder I work the more I love. I rejoice in life for its own sake. Life is no brief candle to me; it is a sort of splendid torch which I've got a hold of for the moment and I want to make it burn as brightly as possible before handing it on to future generations."

—*George Bernard Shaw*[1]

PREPARING FOR THE NEXT EXPEDITION

GUIDEPOSTS

* ✳ Whatever your situation, you have much to offer the people around you.
* ✳ You will grow in your masculine design as you stick to the right path even when it's difficult.
* ✳ God will prepare and equip you with the necessary words and wisdom.

OPEN UP YOUR HANDS

In many ways, this journey has been about you. We set off together on a journey that took us away from the familiar and into the unknown. We have had intense discussions as you have traveled toward true biblical masculinity. I have invited you to offer your influential leadership wherever God has planted you or wherever he may be leading you.

This journey has now reached a point where it is no longer primarily about you. Those things we have discussed along the way must not be forgotten. I have not mentioned them merely for your own personal consumption. You need to apply them to your life, but you also need to pass these words along to others. Jesus has said, "From everyone who has been given much, much will be demanded; and from the one who has been entrusted with much, much more will be asked" (Luke 12:48).

Do not think you have nothing to offer. You have more to give than you might assume. I was recently reminded of this by my pastor, who held up a clear bag of small toys (matchbox cars, small animals, army men, etc.) as an illustration during a sermon. Each toy had been placed in the offering plate by small children who had opened up their hands and offered God what they had to give. My pastor noted that he keeps this bag of toys on the edge of his desk to remind him not to hold too tightly to the things of this world but to be willing to let go.

Take a good look at what you have. Despite what you might believe, you have things that other people need. Primarily, I am talking about the guidance you might offer. As an educator, I know the one who teaches is the one who learns the most. As you offer others the wisdom entrusted to you, personal growth will also naturally occur.

Your new quest is to look around and see whom you might ask to join you on your journey. I can almost guarantee that someone needs to hear from you and have you show him the way. You can do a great service by leading another on the same path toward manhood that you yourself have been traveling down.

Going down a black diamond mogul trail is exhilarating but also requires careful maneuvering on the troughs and back crests. When I tried it for the first time, I was not at all successful. However, a close friend told me to follow him so he could show me a good line to take as we skied The Face at Suicide Six ski slopes in Vermont. Suddenly, everything changed. I saw how he rode the deep troughs, avoided the icy patches, and handled each bump in front of us. This helped me to avoid another ride down the mountain on my backside.

SIDE BY SIDE

Think of what you know and how much it will benefit someone else. Some follow behind, afraid to venture out, afraid of the risk, afraid they might not measure up or have what it takes to begin, let alone complete, the journey. Is the Lord leading you to a person who can accompany you on the journey you have been taking?

As we examine Jesus' life, we see he was very intentional about whom he chose to pursue and to disciple. In Luke 6:12–13, we see Jesus praying the whole night about the choices he was about to make. As he called his disciples to him, he chose twelve men. Even within that group, he focused on an inner core of friends: Peter, James, and John.

As you consider your own choice, let's look back at the prerequisites for beginning a mentorship laid out in chapter 3: Does the person have a teachable and trainable spirit? Is he willing to trust? Does he have an appetite for adventure? Is he open to change? Is he committed? If you have read to this point, it looks like you have done all right yourself!

In Psalm 145:4, David speaks of one generation commending the mighty acts of God to the next. Yet, we cannot leave this task to the "generations," hoping someone else will get the job done. The New Testament gives us a wonderful picture of how Paul took Timothy and mentored him on how to live a godly life. Paul taught him the importance of spreading the gospel for the sake of Christ and his church.

Have a big view of how God can use you. The Devil will try to convince you that you have nothing good to say and are merely wasting your time. Don't listen. Don't be discouraged. Ask God to show you who you are to lead in a mentoring

217

relationship. While Jesus had his Twelve, God may be calling you to make a difference in one life. Be open to the person he brings your way. While I have laid down some guiding criteria, remember God may lead you in a different direction.

Over the years, God has placed young men in my life who did not fit the criteria listed above. At times, I was frustrated because it just didn't seem like they were getting it. However, as someone once said, "A lot of people have gone further than they thought they could because someone else thought they could." Think about it. When someone believed in you and believed you had value and worth and pursued you relentlessly, even if you resisted at first, that confidence may have made all the difference in inspiring you to become the person you are now.

KEEP THE ROLES STRAIGHT

When I felt frustrated by the young men I was guiding, it always helped for me to remember my role. I am not a heart-changer. I am simply a seed-planter with a watering can. If you keep this perspective, you will remember that the Lord of the harvest will change lives. Your role is to be faithful in your calling. After all, the Lord used knuckleheads like Peter in remarkable ways.

When Peter confessed Jesus was the "Christ, the Son of the Living God," our Lord said, "On this rock I will build my church" (Matt. 16:17, 18). As Peter grasped the truth of Jesus' identity, he became not only a powerful and resolute force for the Kingdom of God but was given a discipleship role, directly from Jesus, to "feed my sheep" (John 21:17). Jesus saw through Peter's fiery temper and ready-to-fight attitude to his courageous spirit and impetuous zeal. Jesus knew if that force was channeled, focused, and directed, the church would be on fire for the Lord. He knew Peter's passion, conviction, and rugged spirit were needed for his church.

In fact, the church needed many men like Peter, because it came under stiff persecution following Jesus' ascension into heaven. As Dietrich Bonhoeffer declared, "When Christ calls a man, he bids him to come and die."[2] We are all called to die for various reasons; some, like Peter, are literally called to martyrdom.

So hang in there when you think you are not making a difference. Emerson said, "The whole secret of a teacher's force lies in the conviction that men are convertible."[3] As you help another young man toward biblical manhood, remember the Lord is still teaching and working on you. He has important lessons for you to learn. You never know how he might choose to use you to change a life for eternity.

You may never see the fruit of your labor. However, the Lord may graciously give you a glimpse of a changed heart, a renewed man now living in the light of his glory. I have seen this with my own eyes, and it is a spectacular and dazzling sight to behold. Should you behold it as well, you will realize that every word spoken, every tear shed, every prayer uttered, every conversation shared was completely and utterly for a purpose.

Press on, man! You are on a good path and the right journey!

FINAL THOUGHTS

As I draw to a close, I feel compelled to speak a few concluding thoughts from the wellspring of my heart. I have a vision that, one day, my three sons, Joshua, Josiah, and Jakob, and those "sons" I have spent many years teaching, coaching, and mentoring, as well as other younger "brothers" whom I have not yet had the privilege of meeting will boldly and emphatically declare who they are. May you embrace, pursue, and claim these words:

Keep a clear eye towards life's end. Do not forget your purpose and destiny as God's creature. What you are in his sight is what you are and nothing more. Remember that when you leave this earth, you can take with you nothing that you have received—fading symbols of honor, trappings of power—but only what you have given: a full heart enriched by honest service, love, sacrifice and courage.[4]

May the day soon come when, before your God and alongside your band of brothers, you can claim these honorable virtues and proudly say, with your head held high, "We became *men!*"

DISCUSSION QUESTIONS

1. Consider what God has done in your life through that of another. Some of you have been blessed beyond measure. How might you pass on this blessing and become a blessing to someone else?

2. Has God placed anyone in your life whom you can serve and lead as his "Paul"?

3. If you do not have anyone to lead on this journey, pray that God sends the right person to cross your path. Be open to the person(s) of *his* choosing. That person might be right before you.

4. As you reflect on what you have learned on your own journey thus far, what are the first things you would communicate to the one God places in your life to lead toward biblical manhood? (Consider those things that grabbed your heart and that may have been actually life changing for you.)

REACHING HIGHER

Begin the journey once again—not as a first-time traveler—but as a trail guide blazing the path for another on an adventure of risk, revelation, sacrifice, and service in this great journey toward biblical manhood!

"But the noble man makes noble plans,
and by noble deeds he stands."

—*Isaiah 32:8*

221

RESOURCE LIST:
THE JOURNEY CONTINUES

As you journey on, it is vital for you to keep growing in your understanding and application of biblical manhood. To this end, your local church, youth group, and influential life-mentors will, in God's providence, be of great benefit to you. In addition, below are various resources that you might consider pursuing as a means of growth and grace. While I have given a brief description, I encourage you to check out the websites for additional information.

HERE AND NOW

Young Life. The purpose of this organization is to introduce teens to Jesus Christ and to help them to grow in their faith through authentic friendships.

Focus: high school students/relationships

www.younglife.org

Student Venture. Student Venture is a high school and junior high ministry aimed to lead students into a deeper relationship with Christ. See its website to view their hundred-plus locations around the country.

Focus: high school students/relationships

www.studentventure.org

Christian Service Brigade (CSB Ministries). This is a ministry aimed at the discipleship of young men to develop and hone their leadership abilities. Participants build relationships with Christian men, attend weekly meetings, and learn through hands-on activities.

Focus: discipleship

www.csbministries.org

MISSIONS & ATHLETICS

Fellowship of Christian Athletes (FCA). FCA's purpose, at its absolute core, is to combine people's passion for sports with their passion for Christ and to teach them that those two worlds don't have to be separate. Working in the sporting community to impact the world for Jesus Christ, FCA ministers to those on the inside: the coaches and athletes. The Four Cs of the FCA represent the four branches of its ministry: Coaches, Camp, Campus, and Community.

Focus: athletes

www.fca.org

Athletes in Action (AIA). AIA is a sports ministry designed to use athletics to share the good news of Christ around the world.

Focus: missions using athletics

www.athletesinaction.org

Missionary Athletes International (MAI). The goal of MAI is to "communicate the message of Jesus Christ through the environment of soccer." This is "accomplished by: doing sports ministry, training in sports ministry and deploying sports ministers as a resource to the body of Christ."

Focus: missions using soccer

www.maisoccer.com

TEAMeffort. This interdenominational organization unites teens from different churches in mission trips both in the US and internationally. These involve hard work, Christian outreach, and fun free-day activities.

Focus: mission trips

www.teameffort.org

Mission to the World (MTW). MTW is a mission organization that sends volunteers around the world on missions that can last from one week to many months. Volunteers provide medical aid or disaster relief, help with building, care for street children, etc.

Focus: both short- and long-term missions

www.mtw.org

Youth with a Mission (YWAM). YWAM is an international volunteer movement designed to give youth the training to convey the message of the gospel to those in need. They use music, sports, and performance arts to connect with people of all ages to share of Christ.

Focus: missions

www.ywam.org

MIND AND HEART

Summit Ministries. Through conferences, institutes, blogs, essays, and a multitude of other resources, Summit responds to our current post-Christian culture, challenging Christian youth to stand strong in their faith, defend truth, and prepare youth to have a positive influence on the society in which they live.

Focus: education/mind

www.summit.org

Center for Parent/Youth Understanding: Understanding Culture to Impact Culture (CPYU). CPYU equips teens to deal with the challenge of adolescence through a distinctively Christian worldview and life view. From movie and music reviews to youth culture news and resources, CPYU offers cutting-edge information for teens.

Focus: culture/media

www.cpyu.org

Transform Student Ministries. This organization provides Bible study guides and materials, as well as conferences, seminars, and camps, geared toward helping students study God's word, grow closer to him, and lead others.

Focus: study and knowing God's word

http://www.transformstudent.org

COLLEGE YEARS

Reformed University Fellowship (RUF). This college and university ministry seeks to build a community that reaches students with different beliefs and doubts with the message of the gospel and that equips them to love and serve Jesus and his Church.

Focus: college students

www.ruf.org

InterVarsity Christian Fellowship. This is an evangelical college and university campus ministry. It provides multiethnic ministries, evangelism training, small groups, retreats, and conferences all aimed toward strengthening students in Christ.

Focus: college students

www.intervarsity.org

Navigators. This international, interdenominational ministry has a mission to support those who know and love Jesus while reaching out to people who don't. They provide retreats, conferences, articles, networks for different communities, and more.

Focus: spiritual mentoring/discipleship

www.navigators.org

NOTES

Chapter One: Stay Home?

1. Alex and Brett Harris, *Do Hard Things: A Teenage Rebellion Against Low Expectations* (Colorado Springs, CO: Multnomah Books, 2008), 36.

2. Bernard Iddings Bell. Quoted by W. A. Harper, *Character Building in Colleges* (New York: Abingdon, 1928), 13–14.

Chapter Two: Trail Stories

1. Mark Twain, *The Tragedy of Pudd'nhead Wilson* (Hartford, CT: American Publishing Company, 1894), 77.

2. Napoleon Hill, *Think and Grow Rich* (New York: Textbook Classics, 2011), 13.

3. "Don't Quit," http://www.essentiallifeskills.net/itcouldntbedone .html.

4. "The Passing of the Elves," *The Lord of the Rings: The Fellowship of the Ring: Four-Disc Special Extended Edition*, directed by Peter Jackson (2001; New York, USA: New Line Home Video, 2002), DVD.

Chapter Three: The Trail Guide

1. Robert Lewis, *Raising a Modern-Day Knight: A Father's Role in Guiding His Son to Authentic Manhood* (Carol Stream, IL: Tyndale House, 1997), 2.

2. Larry Crabb, *The Silence of Adam: Becoming Men of Courage in a World of Chaos* (Grand Rapids, MI: Zondervan, 1995), 27.

3. J. C. Ryle, *Thoughts for Young Men* (Amityville, NY: Calvary Press Publishing, 2000), 21.

4. C. S. Lewis, *Of Other Worlds: Essays and Stories* (San Diego, CA: Harvest Books, 2002), 31.

5. Henri Nouwen, "A Spirituality of Waiting," Columbia International University, http://www.ciu.edu/faculty-publications/article /spirituality-waiting.

6. Oswald Chambers, *My Utmost for His Highest* (Westwood, NJ: Barbour and Company, Inc., 1963), 86–87.

7. William Gurnall, *The Christian in Complete Armour* (London, UK: William Tegg, 1862), 299.

Chapter Four: Joined by a Band of Brothers

1. William Shakespeare, *The Life of King Henry the Fifth*, The Oxford Shakespeare, 4.3.65–72, http://www.bartleby.com/70/2943. html.

2. Patrick Morley, *The Man in the Mirror: Solving the 24 Problems Men Face* (Brentwood, TN: Wolgemuth & Hyatt, 1989), 117.

3. Steven Spielberg and Tom Hanks, "Currahee," *Band of Brothers*, season 1, episode 1, directed by Phil Alden Robinson, aired September 09, 2001 (New York City, NY: Warner Brothers, 2002), DVD.

4. Steven Spielberg and Tom Hanks, "Bastogne," *Band of Brothers*, season 1, episode 6, directed by David Leland, aired October 07, 2001 (New York City, NY: Warner Brothers, 2002), DVD.

5. Barack Obama, "The Gallant Story of Salvatore Giunta, America's Newest Medal of Honor Recipient," *Los Angeles Times* speech transcript, November 16, 2010, http://latimesblogs.latimes.com /washington/2010/11/salvatore-giunta-medal-of-honor.html.

6. Ibid.

7. Kim Geiger, "Soldier Is Awarded Medal of Honor," *Los Angeles Times,* November 17, 2010, http://articles.latimes.com/2010/nov/17 /nation/la-na-medal-of-honor-20101117.

8. Henri Nowen, *Out of Solitude: Three Meditations on the Christian Life* (Notre Dame, IN: Ave Maria Press, 1974), 38.

9. Robert Frost, "A Servant to Servants," line 56, http://www .bartleby.com/118/9.html.

10. Bob Herbert, "Reese and Robinson," *The New York Times*, March 14, 1997, http://www.nytimes.com/1997/03/14/opinion /reese-and-robinson.html?src=pm.

11. Harold G. Moore and Joseph L. Galloway, *We Were Soldiers Once . . . and Young* (New York: Random House, 1992), xiv.

12. Steven Spielberg and Tom Hanks, "Points," *Band of Brothers*, season 1, episode 10, directed by Mikael Salomon, aired November 4, 2001 (New York City, NY: Warner Brothers, 2002), DVD.

13. For further discussion of David and Jonathan's uncommon friendship, see Stu Weber, *Tender Warrior: Every Man's Purpose, Every Woman's Dream, Every Child's Hope* (Portland, OR: Multnomoh Books, 1993), 186–198.

14. David W. Smith, *The Friendless American Male* (Ventura, CA: Regal Books, 1983), 15.

Chapter Five: The Wrong Trail

1. Christina Rossetti, "Up-Hill," *Poetry Foundation*, lines 1–4, http://www.poetryfoundation.org/poem/174268.

2. Bernard Madoff, "Full Text: Madoff's Court Statement," *The Associated Press*, March 12, 2009, http://www.cbsnews.com /stories/2009/03/12/business/main4862280.shtml.

3. *I Am a Disciple*, "The Downward Spiral of Sin," article by Jimmy Humphrey, accessed February 01, 2012, http://www.iamadisciple .com/articles/sin.php.

4. J. C. Ryle, *Thoughts for Young Men* (Amityville, NY: Calvary Press Publishing, 2000), 12.

5. Ibid., 14.

6. John Owen, *Triumph In Temptation* (Colorado Springs, CO: Cook Communication Ministries, 2005), 151.

7. "The King's Decision," *The Lord of the Rings: The Two Towers: Four-Disc Special Extended Edition*, directed by Peter Jackson (2002; New York, USA: New Line Home Video, 2003), DVD.

8. J. C. Ryle, *Thoughts for Young Men*, 11.

9. C. S. Lewis, *Mere Christianity* (New York: HarperCollins, 2001), 197.

10. J. R. R. Tolkien, *The Lord of the Rings: The Return of the King* (New York: Ballantine Books, 1954), 100.

Chapter Six: Standing at the Trailhead

1. John Rosemond, *Parenting by the Book: Biblical Wisdom for Raising Your Child* (New York, NY: Howard Books, 2007), 174.

2. Alex and Brett Harris, *Do Hard Things: A Teenage Rebellion Against Low Expectations* (Colorado Springs, CO: Multnomah Books, 2008), 29.

3. Lev Grossman, "Grow Up? Not So Fast," *Time,* January 16, 2005, http://www.time.com/time/magazine/article/0,9171,1018089,00.html.

4. John Rosemond, *Parenting by the Book*, 80.

5. Douglas Bond, *HOLD FAST in a Broken World* (Phillipsburg, NJ: P&R Publishing, 2008), 89.

Chapter Seven: Backcountry Adventures

1. Louis L'Amour, *Ride the Dark Trail* (New York City, NY: Bantam Books, 2010), 53.

2. Harris Interactive, "Video Game Addiction: 81% of American Youth Play; 8.5% are Addicted," http://www.metrics2.com/blog/2007/04/04/video_game_addiction_81_of_american_youth_play_85.html.

3. Don Reisinger, "Halo: Reach Tallies $200 Million on Launch Day," CNET, September 14, 2010, http://news.cnet.com/8301-13506_3-20016658-17.html.

4. Barbara Ortutay, "Video Game Sales Top $21 Billion in 2008," MSNBC, January 15, 2009, http://www.msnbc.msn.com/id/28682836/ns/technology_and_science-games/.

5. John Calvin, *Letters of John Calvin Compiled from the Original Manuscripts and Edited with Historical Notes,* Jules Bonnet, ed. (Philadelphia, PA: Presbyterian Board of Publication, 1858), 416–17.

6. John F. MacArthur, *First Corinthians: New Testament Commentary* (Chicago: The Moody Bible Institute, 1984), 215.

7. Andrew Murray, *Absolute Surrender* (Chicago: Moody Bible Press, 1897), 123.

8. C. S. Lewis, *Mere Christianity* (New York: HarperCollins, 2001), 225.

Introduction to Essential Trail Conversations

1. Henry D. Thoreau, *Walden: A Fully Annotated Edition*, Jeffrey S. Cramer, ed. (New Haven: Yale University Press, 2004), 88.

Chapter Eight: Position versus Performance

1. Collin Welland, *Chariots of Fire*, directed by Hugh Hudson (New York City, NY: Warner Home Video, 1992), videocassette (VHS), 124 min.

2. Ibid.

3. Sarah Julien, "Coming Home: Adoption in Ephesians and Galatians," *Quodlibet Journal* 5, no. 2–3 (2003): http://www.quodlibet .net/articles/murray-adoption.shtml.

Chapter Nine: What's in Your Backyard?

1. C. S. Lewis, "From The Weight of Glory and Other Addresses," *Essential C. S. Lewis*, Lyle W. Dorsett, ed. (New York, NY: Touchstone, 1988), 363. Emphasis in the original.

2. D. M. Lloyd-Jones, *Life In Christ* (Wheaton, IL: Crossway Books, 2002), 14.

3. Timothy Keller, *Counterfeit Gods: The Empty Promises of Money, Sex, and Power, and the Only Hope That Matters* (New York: Dutton, 2009), xviii.

4. J. C. Ryle, *Thoughts for Young Men* (Amityville, NY: Calvary Press Publishing, 2000), 10.

5. Timothy Keller, *Counterfeit Gods*, xviii.

Chapter Ten: Just before the Fall

1. Thomas à Kempis, *The Imitation of Christ* (New York: Vintage Books, 1998), 174.

2. C. S. Lewis, *Mere Christianity* (New York: HarperCollins, 2001), 122.

3. Ibid., 125.

4. J. C. Ryle, *Thoughts for Young Men* (Amityville, NY: Calvary Press Publishing, 2000), 22.

5. "Allen Iverson News Conference Transcript," *Sports Illustrated*, May 10, 2002, http://sportsillustrated.cnn.com/basketball /news/2002/05/09/iverson_transcript/.

6. John Piper, "The Mind of Christ: Looking out for the Interests of Others," Desiring God video excerpt 2:56, August 31, 2008, http://www.desiringgod.org/resource-library/sermons/the-mind-of-christ-looking-out-for-the-interests-of-others#/listen/excerpt.

Chapter Eleven: No Paybacks?

1. Tim Keller, *The Reason for God: Belief in an Age of Skepticism* (New York: Dutton, 2008), 196.

2. Lewis B. Smedes, *Forgive and Forget: Healing the Hurts We Don't Deserve* (San Francisco: Harper Collins Publishers, 1984), 130.

3. John Newton, "A Guide to Godly Disputation," IIIM Magazine Online, 4.27, July 10–July 17, 2002, http://thirdmill.org/newfiles/joh_newton/PT.Newton.godly.disputation.pdf.

4. Tim Keller, *The Reason for God*, 186.

5. Lewis Smedes, *The Art of Forgiving: When You Need To Forgive and Don't Know How* (New York: Ballantine Books, 1996), 147.

6. AT&T, "Silent Treatment," Television commercial, 2012, http://www.youtube.com/watch?v=m5ZeNZtvACI.

7. Lewis Smedes, *The Art of Forgiving*, 171.

8. Anthony Peckham, "Forgiveness Starts Here," *Invictus*, directed by Clint Eastwood, 2009 (New York, NY: Warner Home Video, 2010), DVD.

9. Ibid.

10. Philip Yancey, *Rumors of Another World: What on Earth Are We Missing?* (Grand Rapids, MI: Zondervan, 2003), 223–24.

11. Lewis Smedes, "CT Classic: Forgiveness—The Power to Change the Past," *Christianity Today*, January 07, 1983, http://christianitytoday.com/ct/2002/decemberweb-only/12-16-55.0.html.

Chapter 12: Entertain Me—Now!

1. Sam Storm, *Pleasures Evermore*, (Colorado Springs, CO: NavPress, 2000), 50.

2. Chris Smith, "Super Bowl Commercials Are All Bang, No Buck," *Forbes*, February 03, 2012, http://www.forbes.com/sites/chrissmith /2012/02/03/super-bowl-commercials-are-all-bang-no-buck/.

3. Max Picard, *The World of Silence* (Washington, D.C.: Gateway Editions, 1988), 71.

4. G. K. Chesterton, *Orthodoxy* (San Francisco: Ignatius Press, 1908), 65.

Chapter 13: Flaming Darts

1. Thomas Watson, *The Lord's Prayer* (Rockford, IL: Banner of Truth, 2009), 241.

2. William Gurnall, *The Christian in Complete Armour, or, A Treatise of the Saints' War Against the Devil, Wherein a Discovery Is Made of That Grand Enemy of God and His People, in His Policies, Power, Seat of His Empire, Wickedness, and Chief Design He Hath Against the Saints* (London, UK: Richard Baynes, 1821), iv, http://www.archive.org/stream /christianincompl00gurnuoft#page/n3/mode/2up.

3. Cornelius Van Til, *Essays on Christian Education* (Phillipsburg, NJ: P&R Publishing Company, 1979), 27.

4. Richard J. Krejcir, "Statistics on Pastors," *Schaeffer Institute*, accessed February 14, 2012, http://www.intothyword.org/articles _view.asp?articleid=36562&columnid.

5. John Owen, *The Works of John Owen, Vol. XV*, Thomas Russell, ed. (London: printed for Richard Baynes, 1826), 305.

6. D. L. Moody, *Life Words* (London: John Snow & Co., 1875), 53.

7. Sam Storms, "Tactics of Temptation," *Enjoying God Ministries*, November 8, 2006, http://www.enjoyinggodministries.com/article /tactics-of-temptation/.

8. Thomas Watson, *The Lord's Prayer*, 235.

9. Billy Sunday, quoted in William T. Ellis, *"Billy" Sunday: The Man and His Message* (Philadelphia, PA: The John C. Winston Company, 1914), 79.

10. John Piper, "Satan Uses Sexual Desire," *Desiring God*, December 9, 1984, http://www.desiringgod.org/resource-library/sermons /satan-uses-sexual-desire.

11. Charles Henry Brent, *With God in the World: A Series of Papers* (New York: Longmans, Green, & Co., 1902), 49–50.

Chapter Fourteen: The Daughters of Eve

1. Gary Smalley, *The Joy of Committed Love: A Valuable Guide to Knowing, Understanding, and Loving Each Other* (Grand Rapids, MI: Zondervan, 1984), 179.

2. Ibid.

3. C. S. Lewis, *The Screwtape Letters* (San Francisco: HarperCollins Publisher, 1996), 96.

4. "Many Teens Regret Having Sex," ICR, June 30, 2000, http://www.icrsurvey.com/Study.aspx?f=NatCam_Teens_Regret.html.

5. Fyodor Dostoevsky, *The Brothers Karamazov* (New York: Farrar, Straus, & Giroux, 2002), 108.

Chapter 15: An Invitation to Lead

1. Woodrow Wilson, "The Power of Christian Young Men," *President Wilson's Addresses*, George McLean Harper, ed. (New York: Henry Holt and Company, 1918), 112.

2. *Dictionary.com*, s.v. "leadership," accessed January 31, 2012, http://dictionary.reference.com/browse/leadership.

3. Theodore Roosevelt, "The Man in the Arena," *Almanac of Theodore Roosevelt*, accessed Feb. 15, 2012, http://www.theodore-roosevelt.com/images/research/speeches/maninthearena.pdf.

4. Woodrow Wilson, "The Power of Christian Young Men," 107–8.

5. Jim Elliot, *The Journals of Jim Elliot*, Elisabeth Elliot, ed. (Old Tappan, NJ: Revell, 1978), 174.

6. "Pat Tillman," Biography.com, accessed February 01, 2012, http://www.biography.com/people/pat-tillman-197041.

7. Robert Frost, "The Road Not Taken," *Poetry Foundation*, lines 18–20.

Chapter 16: Preparing for the Next Expedition

1. George Bernard Shaw, Speech at Municipal Technical College and School of Art, Brighton (1907), *Wist: Wish I'd Said That!*,

added March 09, 2009, http://wist.info/shaw-george-bernard/6887/. Emphasis in original.

2. Dietrich Bonhoeffer, *Cost of Discipleship* (New York: Touchstone, 1995), 11.

3. Ralph Waldo Emerson, *Journals of Ralph Waldo Emerson 1820–1872: with Annotations, Vol. 3*, Edward Waldo Emerson and Waldo Emerson Forbes, eds. (Boston and New York: Houghton Mifflin Company, 1910), 278.

4. Loose adaptation of Francis of Assisi, "Letter to the Rulers of the Peoples," Randall Butisingh's weblog, November 5, 2007, http://randallbutisingh.wordpress.com/2007/11/05/thought-for-today-5/.